SPANISH LESSONS

SPANISH LESSONS

CINEMA AND TELEVISION IN CONTEMPORARY SPAIN

Paul Julian Smith

berghahn
NEW YORK · OXFORD
www.berghahnbooks.com

Published in 2017 by
Berghahn Books
www.berghahnbooks.com

Library of Congress Cataloging-in-Publication Data

Names: Smith, Paul Julian author.

Title: Spanish lessons : cinema and television in contemporary Spain / Paul Julian Smith.

Description: New York : Berghahn Books, 2017. | Includes bibliographical references and index.

Identifiers: LCCN 2017016590 (print) | LCCN 2017033762 (ebook) | ISBN 9781785331091 (e-book) | ISBN 9781785331084 (hardback : alk. paper)

Subjects: LCSH: Motion pictures--Spain--History--20th century. | Motion pictures--Spain--History--21st century. | Television programs--Spain--History--20th century. | Television programs--Spain--History--21st century.

Classification: LCC PN1993.5.S7 (ebook) | LCC PN1993.5.S7 S525 2017 (print) | DDC 791.43094609/04--dc23

LC record available at https://lccn.loc.gov/2017016590

British Library Cataloguing in Publication Data

A catalogue record for this book is available from the British Library

ISBN 978-1-78533-108-4 hardback
ISBN 978-1-78533-109-1 ebook

Contents

Illustrations

Acknowledgements

This book is dedicated once more to the faculty and students of the Hispanic and Luso-Brazilian Program at the Graduate Center, City University of New York, who have provided such a fruitful environment in which to teach and write. My thanks are also due to the scholars who kindly invited me to speak in Europe and the Americas, thus providing the initial impetus to write the chapters of this book. I am deeply grateful also to my research assistant Lily Ryan who compiled the final composite bibliography.

Chapters 2 and 4 were first published in *Studies in Spanish and Latin American Cinemas*. Chapter 3 was first published in Marvin D'Lugo and Kathleen M. Vernon (eds.), *A Companion to Pedro Almodóvar* (Oxford: Blackwell, 2013).

New York, September 2015

Introduction
Film, Television, Transmedia

This book is the first to evaluate contemporary Spanish cinema and television in the new context of transmedia, perhaps the most pressing problem in current media studies. It is divided into three sections – film, television, and transmedia – of three chapters each. The aim here, as elsewhere in my work, is to go beyond the limits of Spanish cinema studies, which tends to restrict itself to a small number of art or auteur feature films that are by no means representative of the field as a whole. Moreover, Spanish TV studies, which is practiced only within Spain and in departments of communication and social sciences, focuses on institutional questions and rarely examines concrete texts, as I do here.

In the first part of the book, "Film," chapter 1 begins with a close study of some forgotten feature films from 1980s cinema, a neglected decade; the second chapter gives an account of a festival-cum-industry screening attended by the author; the third explores the media self-fashioning of Spain's best known auteur, Pedro Almodóvar. The second section of the book, on television, gives a detailed report on one full season of series production (chapter 4), an analysis of LGBT dramas in Catalonia (chapter 5), and an account (chapter 6) of three TV series on the construction boom and bust that has caused Spaniards such anguish and is perhaps the country's most pressing social issue. The third and final section of the book, which also contains three chapters, first traces the little known history of the crossover between cinema and television since the 1950s (chapter 7). Chapter 8 moves to the present, proposing a new paradigm in the Spanish audiovisual scene, one that inverts historical hierarchies: namely, popular cinema and quality television. Chapter 9 presents a transmedia study of current fiction on the economic crisis, offering close readings of case studies in print, cinema, and TV. Fittingly for a study of transmedia, this last chapter shows how the novel and television have become more cinematic, while cinema has become more televisual.

The central focus of the book is, as its title suggests, the question of education. And there is a strong current of pedagogy in Spanish discourse around cinema and, perhaps surprisingly, television. Such an educational mission is of course to be defined very broadly. Thus one specialized book posits an essential "relation of conflict" between culture and media, with the former defined restrictedly as ever-threatened television arts programming (Rodríguez Pastoriza 2003). Conversely the best TV blogger in Spain defends Spanish fiction series, which often choose a historical subject, as sources of learning, thus radically expanding the realm of pedagogy. As the pseudonymous "Chica de la tele" ("TV Girl") writes, we need to ask ourselves the question: "What is a cultural program?" Her example here is *El ministerio del tiempo* ("The Ministry of Time," TVE, 2015), an innovative science fiction series that managed to turn Golden Age luminaries Velázquez and Lope de Vega into trending topics on Twitter (Chica de la Tele 2015).

In a rare reference to television in his *Distinction*, Bourdieu cites highbrow cultural programing as "part of the paraphernalia which always announces the sacred character, separate and separating, of high culture" (1996, 34). The blurring of boundaries and leveling of distinctions promised by transmedia and newly complex TV render such a position untenable.

This extension of the educational or didactic beyond traditional limits is a theme that, in a transmedia variant, echoes throughout this book. Thus, according to one scholar, the films of the 1980s that I discuss in the first chapter embody two didactic missions. The first is to present classics of Spanish literature through an accessible form and high production values; the second is to emphasize the hardship of life in the postwar period, but without apportioning blame for that deprivation. Cultural and political pedagogy here come together in a middlebrow cinema that educates Spaniards in the new rights and responsibilities of democracy.

The industry screenings and movie market known as "Madrid de Cine," which I examine in the second chapter, also prove to be a perhaps unexpected classroom. The press conferences I report on here sought to educate foreign correspondents on the nature of Spanish cinema (which earns twice as much income abroad as it does at home), while the films themselves embraced new trends such as postapocalyptic thrillers, literate ensemble pieces, genre pieces, auteur movies, and technically innovative features. What is striking, however, is that it is the popular cinema shown to buyers and critics in Madrid de Cine (most especially science fiction, a rare genre in Spain) that offers the clearest and most resonant lessons on the nation's present situation, on its economic decline and environmental degradation.

The third chapter begins by addressing the new configuration of art, industry, and auteurs in a context where media-savvy directors have learned lessons on how to conjugate the uncanny combination of personal intimacy and physical distance characteristic of social media. In its second half the chapter charts how Almodóvar, a director openly concerned with pedagogy in films such as *La mala educación* ("Bad Education," 2004), fails to adapt to a new, less forgiving and respectful media landscape. Nonetheless he seeks to refine his own image and connect with a newly slippery audience in such self-reflexive mediations on the artistic and industrial process as *Los abrazos rotos* ("Broken Embraces," 2009), the main subject of the chapter.

Even more so than film, television has been seen by scholars in Spain as raising the question of education. Indeed Manuel Palacio, the doyen of TV historians, claims social "pedagogy" as a key term in the development of a medium often still dismissed as trash ("telebasura") (2001, passim). My fourth chapter, which is parallel to my second on the annual crop of film shown at Madrid de Cine, explores the unusually rich spring season of television fiction in 2009, placing it in the context of migration between the two media of film and TV and the continuing importance of cultural proximity in an era of transnational production. Beginning with a survey of the current TV ecology, it goes on to evaluate four innovative and popular titles: miniseries *23F: El día más difícil del Rey* ("February 23: The King's Most Difficult Day") and series *Águila Roja* ("Red Eagle"), *Pelotas* ("Balls") (all from Televisión Española), and *Doctor Mateo* (Antena 3), a rare adaptation of a British format. This chapter argues that these fictions share three themes: a continuing exploration of Spanish national history, both distant and recent; the fractured family, particularly as caused by missing mothers; and nostalgia for close community, whether its location is urban or rural. While such nostalgia might seem reactionary, combined with the previous themes (which are more evidently educational), the mourning for a lost past can serve as a kind of social pedagogy for the alienated modern nation.

Chapter 5, the second chapter on television, discusses LGBT fiction series in Catalonia. Starting with a major feature film by the country's best-known director that laid the foundations for such representations, the chapter goes on to argue that the goal of long-form fiction (especially when it is funded, as here, by a public service broadcaster) is to work through social issues such as homosexuality, guiding audiences toward pedagogic objectives. Indeed, in an interview Josep Maria Benet i Jornet, the prestigious playwright who created one of these series, says explicitly that his aim was "to educate the public" in such "unpleasurable" areas as gayness, cancer, and diabetes (a somewhat problematic list) (Barranco 2014). Nonetheless the series in question exploit the closeness to the audience that is especially charged for the TV medium in a smaller nation with a unique language and culture such as Catalonia. Strikingly, this politically progressive pedagogy is found in series set both in the city (Barcelona) and in the more conservative countryside.

Chapter 6, the last and longest chapter on television, examines three series whose plots center around the property bubble of the last decade and its attendant corruption and misery. Here I begin by showing how academic studies of the Spanish real estate sector give their readers lessons in solidarity and sustainability, by critiquing past practices and promoting future development that is less socially and environmentally harmful than before. Turning to the series themselves, we see how they likewise teach negative lessons on harm (a wealthy developer, Croesus-like, destroys all he touches) or positive lessons in caring (a formerly carefree young woman takes responsibility for her dead sister's family). Very diverse in genre, ranging from crazy comedy to tragic drama, these series thus educate Spaniards on the very visible perils of the present and point, implicitly, to the possibilities of a different future that is more difficult to imagine.

Chapter 7, the first on transmedia, considers the forgotten history of crossovers between cinema and television. A telling example is how a single actor in a single year (Lluís Homar in 2009) could play similar characters in a film and a TV serial, fathers who engage in a kind of personal pedagogy with their sons (one of them is a film director, the other the King of Spain). Beyond such textual similarities, I suggest that the well-known virtues of television (its familiarity, domesticity, and cultural closeness to a local audience) might be imitated in a film medium that has sometimes turned its back on national spectators and could learn valuable lessons from the successes of the small screen.

In the eighth chapter I return to the idea of television as a kind of democratic pedagogy in Spain, but now in the context of recent quality or complex TV series. Thus while "televisual" feature films have reconnected with mass audiences via the popular thriller genre, "cinematic" television has asked Spaniards to meditate within the law and justice format on such thorny issues as drug trafficking, colonialism, and Islamist terror. As we shall see, the transparent visual and narrative pleasures of such ambitious television do not undermine but rather reinforce its continuing didactic intent. The key case here is Antena 3's lavish historical miniseries *El tiempo entre costuras* ("The Time In Between," 2013–14).

In the final chapter I return to the theme of crisis, inescapable in Spain, which was discussed earlier in the more restricted field of the property bubble. Here I note textual similarities between a prize-winning novel, feature film, and TV series, all of which propose via their claustrophobic narrative worlds that there is no way out of Spain's current conundrum and that the nation is set on a one-way voyage that permits no return. In the original and creative forms to which they appeal, however, the three texts suggest that Spaniards need not be the prisoners of their history (the term I use for this process is "path dependence"), that rather they can trace new and collective "desire lines" in a postapocalyptic landscape.

I trust that the evidence of the creativity of the Spanish audiovisual sector displayed throughout this book will convince readers also of this final and more positive moral. In spite or perhaps because of a crisis that is at once economic, political, and cultural, Spain has, as we shall see, experienced a continuing emergence of new and complex artistic phenomena arising from the multiple interactions of transmedia.

As will be evident from the pages above, in this book I tend to use transmedia as the mutual relation or coexistence of multiple media in a single text or institution: thus the feature films of the 1980s incorporate the literary values or the television aesthetic of the period, while, conversely, the television series of the millennium aspire to the production values once monopolized by cinema. Beyond these empirical relationships, transmedia (and its related term "intermedia") also suggest new historical and theoretical approaches to diverse cultural objects.

One compelling account of the subject is Agnes Petho's "Intermediality in Film: A Historiography of Methodologies." Petho starts by addressing the continuing suspicion of a term that remains perilously poised between film and media studies, asking whether it is a legitimate scholarly enterprise (2010, unpaginated). Further questions arise: Is intermediality a rift in film theory or just a blind spot? And is film itself, threatened as it is by electronic or digital transmedia, an incredible shrinking medium or an intermedium?

Charting paths along the historical axis, Petho returns to early models of film as synesthetic experience, noting that far from being new, "the idea that cinema is unavoidably interconnected with other media and arts has been a constant issue ... ever since the first moving picture shows were presented in a theatrical environment and ever since movies attempted to present narratives and to produce emotions by a combination of images in movement, music and words." Thus, she writes, Rudolf Arnheim's *New Laocoön* (1938) examines the advent of the talkies by dismissing sound as an unwelcome interference with the purity of the visual medium. Later, however, Arnheim revised his attitude, stating:

> *I see now that there is no such thing as a work limited to a single medium. ... The film medium, as I recognize now, profits from a freedom, a breathing space that I could not afford to consider when I fought for the autonomy of the cinema. ... This freedom puts the film more closely in the company of the other performing arts, such as the theater, the dance, music, or pantomime. (cited by Petho)*

Arnheim turns here, then, to a synesthetic model reminiscent of Wagner's "total work of art" (*Gesamtkunstwerk*).

Petho herself concludes:

> *The mapping of such tendencies has brought the study of cinematic intermediality far from the mere listing of media combinations or analogies of intertextual relations. ... There has been, in general, a major shift from the utopia of the* Gesamtkunstwerk *to the heterotopia of intermediality.*

Petho's discussion thus provides a prelude to the three chapters on film that begin this book. For if cinema has always been made up of multiple media (a rich mix of Arnheim's theater, dance, music, and pantomime), then, newly challenged as it is by television and the internet, film deserves to be read not as a utopian fusion but as a heterotopic combination of those distinct elements.

PART I

Film

CHAPTER 1

Spanish Cinema of the 1980s
Two Approaches, Four Films

Two Approaches: The Social and the Cultural

This first chapter attempts to lay a theoretical foundation for studying Spanish film by giving an account of two major studies of Spanish cinema in the 1980s, which call themselves respectively "social" and "cultural." It goes on to relate those studies to four neglected films that were chosen by a team of scholars at Madrid's Carlos III University as representative of the decade. The main questions asked are: What is the nature of periodization in such an academic project? And to what extent do the characteristics of the neglected corpus of unstudied films coincide with those of the better-known works of the decade on which critics have based their accounts?

As we shall see, there is by no means a consensus over 1980s Spanish cinema as an object of research; and, yet, the case studies here, representative of the dark continent of feature films that fail to benefit from either popular or academic favor, do reconfirm some academic judgments on the period. Yet there is something bracingly uncanny in watching titles that are at once so strange and so familiar.

Sally Faulkner's *A History of Spanish Film* (2013) is subtitled "Cinema and Society 1910–2010." Unlike other critics, Faulkner does believe that the 1980s constitutes a distinct period and thus devotes a separate chapter to it, even as she refers in passing to the Transition as a more accepted, albeit still contested and ill-defined, temporal marker. The title of the chapter reveals her novel interpretative focus, citing the cinema sponsored by the director general of film appointed by the new Socialist government: "Miró Films and the Middlebrow Cinema in the 1980s."

Faulkner begins by covering familiar ground, noting that the political debate on continuity or change at the start of the decade can also be applied to "Spanish film historiography" (2013, 160). Thus, in spite of the tardy and self-interested adoption of the director by the establishment, models of rupture tend to cluster around Almodóvar, whose *Pepi, Luci, Bom* was released in 1980. What Faulkner dubs "Mirovian" cinema is also contradictory in its reception. While a few scholars praise the novelty of this "quality cinema, with high budgets, a preference for literary adaptations, and an eye for international distribution and festivals" (2013, 161), many others cite these same characteristics as continuous with the so-called "New Spanish Cinema" sponsored under late Francoism in the 1960s and the Third Way films of the 1970s (2013, 162). English-speaking critics especially tend to condemn Miró's legislation for "cronyism, for its imposition of a uniform, politicized view of Spanish culture and for … shrinking the variety of output and stifling in particular its popular, commercial trends" (2013, 161). Faulkner argues, to the contrary, for "sympathetic attention" to this branch of cinema and a reassessment of "the ways these films lie in-between art and popular trends" (2013, 163). Crucially she notes here a convergence with TV, where the middle-class audience was also served by the rise of "filmic" quality television serials (2013, 163).

With this polemical intent and deliberately restricted focus, Faulkner proposes a corpus of six films for the close analyses that take up the great bulk of her chapter: Trueba's urban comedy Ópera prima ("Opera Prima,"1980); Saura's dance drama *Bodas de Sangre* ("Blood Wedding," 1981); Camus's period piece *La colmena* ("The Beehive," 1982); Betriú's Barcelona-set *La plaça del Diamant* ("The Time of the Doves," also 1982); and finally Fernán Gómez's political comedy *Mambrú se fue a la guerra* ("Mambru Went to War") and Gutiérrez Aragón's *La mitad del cielo* ("Half of Heaven," both 1986) (2013, 164). Faulkner is at once aware of the diversity of genre in this corpus and anxious to find similarities between the works, based on a flexible definition of her chosen tool, the middlebrow. Thus she says of the last pair of films, "Working in the very different idioms of comedy and melodrama [they] find a means to address the past and relate it to the present that is both intelligent and accessible" (2013, 164). Three of her films are also literary adaptations, the subject of Faulkner's first monograph.

Along these lines, Ópera prima is thus read as treading a thin line between farce and a more subtle comedy of manners (2013, 165). High production values (even on a tiny budget), a literate script, and skilled actors combine in the service of a relatively subversive new theme: the crisis of masculinity (2013, 166). Moreover, Trueba combines cinephile high- and low-brow references (Godard and pornography) in a way that (unlike the more challenging postmodern approach) "fuses its plural intertexts" (2013, 167). This finely tuned balance is at once formal and ideological: the film is "well crafted" but muted in its social satire, with women serving their traditional function as "vessels to work through social change" in what remains a "heterosexual male fantasy," albeit conjoined with a "youthful experimental spirit" (2013, 168).

As Faulkner acknowledges, the juxtaposition of this jokey, talky Madrid comedy with an austere (and mute) flamenco ballet is "jarring" (2013, 168). Specificities of place and time are now stripped away and respect required for a "holy trinity of revered left-wing intellectuals": Saura, Gades, and Lorca (2013, 169). Yet just as Trueba upgrades sex farce, Saura upgrades the folkloric Francoist musical. Often criticized by academics (or, conversely, redeemed by an appeal to auteurism problematic in this middlebrow context), *Bodas de sangre* receives once more a "sympathetic" treatment from Faulkner, who highlights the role of producer Emiliano Piedra and his "didactic mission to present classics of Spanish literature ... through an accessible form and high production values" (2013, 171). Once more this process is both formal and ideological. Lorca's play is "pared down," with the central (unspoken) metaphor of "submission to the rules and rigors of dance" standing in for a repressive society (171). In the mise-en-scène, the dance studio mirror represents this disciplinary process (2013, 172). And just as popular flamenco music is paired with high-art ballet, so former Francoist child star Marisol is made to share the frame with the "tortured" steps of a dancer. The role of the middlebrow here, then, is to rescue Saura's dance trilogy from critics' insistence on auteurism, placing these films in a wider social context and raising the possibility of "two Sauras," both of which deserve sympathetic attention (2013, 173).

Faulkner is less forgiving of Camus. While *La colmena* can be read (like *Bodas*) in Bourdieu's terms as an "attempt to acquire cultural capital through the short-cut of a film adaptation" (2013, 176), it uses middlebrow resources (high-culture references and production values, revered actors) in a way inconsistent with its chosen genre. Thus "refined mise en scene sabotages, rather than enhances, ... social realism" (2013, 177). What is important here, however, is that Faulkner is not repeating the traditional complaints made by "fidelity criticism" of unfaithfulness to a more complex and disturbing original or the puritan critiques of those hostile to overpleasing Mirovian aesthetics. Rather she is suggesting that, in spite of *La colmena*'s popular and critical success, form and content fail to converge here in a strictly cinematic way (177).

La plaça del Diamant was also attacked on its release, in this case by critics such as José Luis Monterde, as a triple threat: middlebrow, period, and a literary adaptation (2013, 178). Faulkner's close reading attempts, however, to rescue a film made, like *La colmena*, in coproduction with TVE (2013, 178). While Betriú's project did indeed appeal to the literary prestige of Rodoreda (her image appears in the credits), the politics of his adaptation was ambiguous ("a didactic mission to emphasize hardship but not apportion blame" [2013, 179]) and his use of film form crucial. Faulkner cites here five key elements: audio track, cinematography, mise-en-scène, editing, and casting (2013, 180). Some challenging techniques (colored filters, direct address to camera) combine to form an effect that is "serious, if not provocative," "accessible and thought-provoking" (184), emblematic of the middle path.

With *Mambrú*, on the other hand, Fernán Gómez "plays the past off against the present" (2013, 86), opposing the materialism of the 1980s to the idealism of the 1930s (2013, 187). But he does so (like Betriú) using filmic technique: the metaphor of light and vision arises from the weakened eyes of the "topo" (literally "mole") hero, who has spent forty years in hiding during the Francoist regime. Felt to be a literal "burden" by his family, he is in one sequence carried through the streets by them (2013, 188). Unlike in Berlanga, however, "comic treatment is light rather than grotesque" and political perspective equally nuanced, suggesting "a sly irreverence towards the Socialist government that subsidized [the film]" (2013, 189).

With her final film, *La mitad del cielo*, Faulkner also "balances contextual questions with close textual analysis" in an equilibrium worthy of her chosen middlebrow theme (2013, 190). Here genre is complex, merging biopic, chronicle of migration, Francoist history, and feminism. Yet this "interpretative multiplicity" is combined with accessible treatment (2013, 191). Employing food as a mediation for less palatable politically significant themes, the film's anti-Francoism and feminism are both relatively muted (2013, 192) and sweetened by high production values and accessible high-culture references (one set-up mirrors Velásquez's *Las meninas* [2013, 193]). Avoiding once more an auteurist reading, Faulkner attributes the success of *La mitad* above all to Ángela Molina, whose "unfussy" performance redeems a potentially implausible "feminist fairy tale" (2013, 196).

At the end of this summary, we might object that the middlebrow is at once too broad and too narrow as an interpretative tool for a social reading of Spanish cinema of the 1980s. On the one hand, it is so capacious a category as to embrace films that appear to have little in common (from the comedy of manners to the po-faced literary adaptation); on the other, it restricts those films to a single role (that of mediating between low and high culture). In my view, however, the value of this approach is that it permits the reevaluation of a body of work frequently dismissed out of hand by critics, both Spanish- and English-speaking; and it permits the theorization at a certain level of abstraction of concrete changes in production and distribution during the period. For example the rise in budgets and production values on the one hand and the decline in mass cinema audiences on the other come together in the creation and reception of texts that aspire to a new level of cultural capital.

Moreover, these industrial factors (Faulkner offers figures for government subsidies and ticket revenue) can be integrated with the aesthetic techniques (plush mise-en-scène, nuanced performance style) that were recognized by both filmmakers and filmgoers as intrinsic to this new mode of cinema. Faulkner thus goes beyond Bourdieu's social critique of the class basis of taste to offer (unlike the French sociologist) formal analyses and value judgments of her chosen cultural field.

The title of Vicente J. Benet's *El cine español: una historia cultural* (2012) is teasingly close to Faulkner's (with the substitution of "cultural" for "social"). Yet his book's account of the 1980s could hardly be more different in periodization or approach. To start with Benet displays a cavalier indifference to the orderly procession of decades observed by Faulkner, appealing rather to multiple and overlapping periods that ignore even such political landmarks as the Civil War, Dictatorship, and the Transition to democracy. Thus chapter 5 ("Looking Outside") extends from 1951 to 1970, chapter 6 ("Eccentric Paths") from 1925 to 1980, and chapter 7 ("The Establishment of Modernity") from 1968 to 1996. Even within this last chapter Benet does not stick to chronological order, jumping instead between genres and ending with the *quinqui* (teenage gangster) cinema of the late 1970s and early 1980s (400–402). Likewise, Almodóvar's *Pepi, Luci, Bom* (treated conventionally by Faulkner as the beginning of a new cinematic period) is here claimed (with Iván Zulueta's *Arrebato* ["Rapture," 1979]) as the end of experimental film in Spain: "the end of the road, ... the final follower of an experimental, independent, or marginal cinema that had established a parallel path to that of commercial film since the time of the historic avant-gardes" (2012, 358).

Benet's history, as exceptional in a Spanish context as Faulkner's is in the context of Anglophone scholarship, won a prize from the Academia de Cine in 2013. A press report on the ceremony wrote that the book "sets out an approach to Spanish cinema not as an isolated phenomenon but as the expression of a cultural industry integrated into the country's processes of social and political transformation." It went on to add that it treats "an art that has reflected the processes of social change, the historical events produced by Spain's integration into modernity, not to mention the dialogue and connection with literature, painting, music, theater, and radio" (note the absence of television in this list), and analyzes some three hundred films. How, then, does Benet address the industrial, sociopolitical, and transmedia aspects of Spanish film in the 1980s?

Curiously, perhaps, the decade figures little in the various sections of the one chapter whose temporal limits embrace it. "Times of Memory" examines four documentaries of the 1970s (2012, 359–66); "Aesthetics of Repression" covers two styles in fiction films of the same decade, the "symbolism" of Saura and Erice and the "tremendismo" (expressionistic distortion) of Franco and Borau. Benet cites Gutiérrez Aragón on the "decomposition" of a model that would drag on through the early 1980s: "the progressive dissolution of these stylistic brands of the 70s towards more linear plotlines, albeit with the survival of some glimmers of some of them, in both mise en scene and the description of unsettling family scenes" (2012, 374). "Chronicle of the Present" cites briefly some movies of the early 1980s rated "S" (for "sex") (2012, 375–76) before retreating to a mash-up of Garci, Bardem, Landa, de la Iglesia, Berlanga, Pons, and Bigas Luna mostly at the end of the previous decade (2012, 376–78). "A Country on the Move" returns to the "hedonism" of *Pepi, Luci* and *Arrebato* in 1979–80 (2012, 391–92) before skipping to Bigas Luna's *Huevos de oro* ("Golden Balls") in 1993 (2012, 394–95).

Just two pages are then devoted to the cinema enabled by the Miró Law of 1983, including brief references to several of the titles cited by Faulkner (*La plaça del Diamant, La colmena*) (2012, 397). Benet's short account is more disinterested than hostile, citing such films' "good academic quality" and success in "laying the foundations of the current audiovisual industry" (2012, 398). Before the peroration on *quinqui* cinema, a final sketch treats film from the *autonomías* (self-governing regions), starting with the appearance of local TV stations in 1983–84 and noting that even by that time Basque films such as Imanol Uribe's *La muerte de Mikel* ("Michael's Death," 1984) or the later *Vacas* (Julio Medem, 1992) were no longer epic, celebratory, or victimist but rather critical of the nationalist project (2012, 399).

While Benet's rejection of linear chronology is potentially revelatory, his version of the 1980s is wholly negative in character. The decade thus lacks both the exploration of historical memory and repression and the urgency of the present, which are curiously both traced back to the 1970s. Conversely the Mirovian cinema of the 1980s is valued, as we have seen, mainly for its industrial role in preparing for the present. Clearly Benet, unlike Faulkner, also has little interest in close analysis of individual films (as the tally of three hundred discussed in the book would suggest).

Rather, however, the strength of his history is in the references to broad social and institutional questions with which his hop-scotching cinema narrative is studded. Thus the 1970s "aesthetics of repression" (which he claims staggered on into the 1980s) is not merely aesthetic but rather tied to the taste of "influential film festivals and Parisian journals" (2012, 367). Likewise, the symbolic and *tremendista* tendencies are said to be legitimized by "foreign Hispanists," biased toward auteurism, seeking to mark their territory in the university institution, and promoting in the United States a supposed Oedipal pact of forgetting for a period in Spain when in fact "there are few moments of more intense return to the past in cultural products" (2012, 373).

More broadly the "chronicle of the present" is related to "a profound change in values" said to date from as far back as 1968 (2012, 374), according to which cultural products would no longer be valued in terms of artistic tradition but rather through "immediate enjoyment and entertainment, which turned television into the model medium" (2012, 375). Now all media would be mixed and leveled, and there would be no difference between high and low culture. The country that was "moved" in the 1980s, then, was characterized by two cultural "layers": the modern or postmodern (Benet seems to use the terms as synonyms) understood as mass consumption, economic development, and "bringing into line" of Spain with the rest of the advanced world, on the one hand; and the "contestatory" trend of the underground, itself inherited from the 1970s, on the other (2012, 388–89).

Now Benet's acknowledgment of the institutional influence of varied bodies in Spain or abroad (Parisian journals and US universities) is welcome in a Spanish film studies that would rather treat its field as aesthetically autonomous. But his broad-brush account of the (post)modern condition allegedly characteristic of the 1980s is unhelpful. His long process of "establishment of modernity" in Spain may include both the canonic *El espíritu de la colmena* (1973) and the softcore porno *Los sueños húmedos de Patrizia* ("Patrizia's Wet Dreams," 1982). But Benet himself implicitly acknowledges the continuing differences in prestige between the art movies of the auteurs he places in social context and the despised sexploitation and *quinqui* movies he seeks to reappraise. The current audiovisual industry, with its legitimizing apparatus of prizes and academy established precisely in the 1980s, shows precious little evidence of promiscuous mixing and leveling. Indeed the gap between commercial movies and festival films has rarely been wider in Spain than it is today. And the history of television itself, which, as we have seen, embraced "filmic" quality in the 1980s, is hardly immune to processes of cultural distinction and social differentiation.

Benet's stress on the blurring of high and low, however, rewrites in a different key Faulkner's proposal of the middlebrow as a key term for the decade, even as he marginalizes that decade and its Mirovian school in his chapter. And note that Faulkner distinguishes between two kinds of blurring: the reassuring synthesis of diverse elements in Trueba and the more challenging, unresolved juxtapositions in Almodóvar, which truly merit the term "postmodern." My point, then, is that the absence of the 1980s in Benet's history is not random, but structural. His undifferentiated model of the (post)modern as mixing and leveling cannot account for a decade typified, in Faulkner's view, by a precarious balance of high and low culture elements that remain nonetheless culturally legible and aesthetically distinct from one another.

Four Films

Let us look now at the opening sequences of four unsung films of the 1980s according to the conflicting interpretative frameworks sketched above. As none of these features is mentioned by Faulkner or Benet, they will serve as test cases for the generalizability of the latter's models for the decade, which are themselves based on distinct and varied corpuses. The fact that not one of the directors of this new body of work achieved a continuing career after the 1980s also makes them uniquely representative of the decade in which their films were produced. The fact that none of the films is a comedy (unlike in Faulkner's corpus) also suggests that they constitute a relatively coherent body of serious drama.

Brumal (1986) is directed by Cristina Andreu, who also takes a coscreenwriter credit with Cristina Fernández Cubas, the author of the then-recent collection of stories on which the feature was based, *Los altillos de Brumal* (1983). Andreu's feature would seem to come closest to the model of the Mirovian middlebrow presented by Faulkner in which coproduction funding comes from television.

Indeed the first credit reads "Film subsidized by the Ministry of Culture," and a later one "with the collaboration of TVE." The only period picture and literary adaptation in our corpus, it benefits from a literate script, picturesque mise-en-scène, professional production values, and a relatively prestigious cast. Lucia Bosé as the mother, unfortunately dubbed and wigged, brings with her memories of perhaps the most celebrated film of the New Spanish Cinema of the Dictatorship, *Muerte de un ciclista* ("Death of a Cyclist," 1955). A first interior scene, in which the mother braids her young daughter's hair, evokes a very similar sequence in that other hallowed precedent for quality cinema of the 1980s, *El espíritu de la colmena*. Indeed the basic premise here, of the child's uncomprehending vision of the painful legacy of the past, is perhaps the greatest cliché of Spanish film during the extended period of modernization identified by Benet.

In traditional style, the opening shots thus raise multiple enigmas to be resolved in the course of the film. In the credit sequence (exterior, day), the camera cranes down to the daughter and mother, the latter black clad and stone faced, as they wait with their modest luggage by the roadside in a somewhat bleak rural landscape. The pair is accompanied by a plangent piano motif. A teasing close-up of the child's bread and tomato dropped on the asphalt perhaps suggests a Catalan connection that remains unspoken. In the period bus (of what year?) the couple are ostracized by fellow passengers during the journey (for what reason?) and arrive at night in a small town (where?), prettily lit in blue day-for-night. Bosé turns her coat inside out (why, once more?) and speaks the first line of dialogue: "Today we begin a new life." With no exposition or backstory offered, the old life remains shrouded in mystery.

Illustration 1.1: Lucia Bosé in *Brumal* (1986)

The style would thus seem to be reminiscent of the "symbolic" school of the aesthetics of repression, to whose uncanny continuation into the 1980s Benet called attention. And (as in that revision of the earlier period) the treatment here is more linear, even as we are returned to the unsettling family spaces familiar from the 1960s and 1970s. Bosé's mother thus engages in a mysterious phone conversation with her lawyer, in which she discusses continued payments of rent from unknown family property (before crushing a bug beneath her elegant shoe). But if she seems distant, she is by no means the cruel or grotesque matriarch of much post-Franco "memory" film. Nor is Kity Manver as a sharp-suited teacher exceptionally malicious in school scenes that evoke *El espíritu*. Far indeed from "tremendista" brutality, we are, as the opening sequence continues, progressively distanced from the more rigorous enigmas typical of the symbolic school. An explanatory voiceover spoken by the adult daughter (a resource considered but finally omitted by Erice from *El espíritu*, once more) states unambiguously that it is not society but the child who is "different."

In spite of such certainties, time and space remain teasingly abstract: the child is unable to point out Brumal, the hometown with such a mistily evocative name, on the schoolroom map of Spain. And the children's immaculate blue uniforms make period precision equally problematic. Antiquarian art design is reinforced by a further picturesque location: the junk or antique shop stocked with vintage dolls and contraptions where a painter practices his craft. Delicately treading the middlebrow line, Andreu and Fernández Cubas deny spectators the contextualization they might prefer but fail to challenge them with more radical narrative or ideological disruption. Hence, unlike in *La plaça del Diamant*, the polished voiceover is reassuring rather than troubling and there is no direct address to camera. Indeed *Brumal*'s bid for distinction (by and for its little-known first-time female director and screenwriters) derives from the coherence or consistency with which these various technical elements are blended together. It goes without saying that this kind of filmic practice, whose industrial and aesthetic ambitions so evidently aspire to quality, is innocent of that cultural mixing and leveling that Benet ascribes to the (post)modernity that is said to characterize Spain in this decade. It is a kind of filmmaking, intelligent and accessible, that, as Faulkner suggests, deserves to be taken sympathetically on its own, middlebrow terms.

Rather than branding *Brumal* as a Benet-style zombie-like continuation of past practices, we might then stress its 1980s-like renovation of the memory mode. Thus, unlike many literary adaptations of the time, this film is based on a very recent work, one that cannot lay claim to the prestige of past male masters such as Lorca or even Cela as a shortcut to cultural capital for its audience. Conversely and more radically, we can indeed read the film within the context of the feminist frame that Faulkner found in *La mitad del cielo*. Although it does deal with memory and amnesia, themes eminently exploitable for political allegory, *Brumal* focuses instead on female psychology: such a Bildungsroman is implied from the first confident words spoken in the adult woman's voice over the child's image. There is also a prominent reference to Joan of Arc (saint or witch?) in early dialogue, a hint of female heroism and autonomy far indeed from the familiar role of woman as mere mediator of historical change that Faulkner identifies in male-authored film of the 1980s.

Moreover, the focus on relatively benevolent mother-daughter relations works against the heritage of castrating or incestuous mothers of sons to be found in the still recent *tremendista* tradition. Even the mysterious geographical dislocation of the hometown would likely be read by the target quality audience (probably familiar with the literary original) not as a pact of oblivion in the service of a forgetful democracy ("Now we begin a new life") but as a pointer to a popular literary genre: Fernández Cubas was known for her allegiance to the fantastic idiom, whose narrative disruptions are not immediately available for social critique. Working through the past without evident trauma, then, this polished period piece confirms, in spite of initial appearances, that settling of modernity and "bringing into line" of Spain with the advanced world is Benet's great theme of film from 1968 to 1996.

Antxon Ezeiza's *Días de humo/Ke arteko egunak* ("Days of Smoke," shot in 1989, released 1990) shares a mistily evocative title with *Brumal*. And although the first credit we see is for the Filmoteca Vasca, we later read once more that the film is subsidized by Madrid's Ministry of Culture along with Spanish national television. While *Brumal* is defined by the ministry's database as simply a "drama," *Días* is called more precisely a "political drama," perhaps attesting to the Basque origin or male focus of what is once more a late entry in the cycle of memory films. Although Ezeiza (whose name is given in Spanish sources, unlike in the credits here, as "Antonio Eceiza") boasts a varied CV during twenty years before this film, comprising features shot both at home and in exile in Mexico, *Días* attracted an audience of just fifty thousand on its release. Praised as the "father of Basque film" in one obituary (Moreno 2011), he is also described as having a troubled history with both funding bodies and the public.

The opening shot of *Días*, set to a melancholy clarinet motif, is of clouds viewed from a plane, an evident symbol of displacement. We hear a flight attendant announcing arrival in "the autonomous community of Euskadi" and welcoming those passengers returning (like Ezeiza himself) after so many years abroad. In this case it is with "Operación añoranza" ("Operation Nostalgia" or "Homesickness"), a scheme funding the temporary visits of exiles to the various parts of the Spanish state where they were born. As the plane lands at the characteristically cloudy Bilbao airport, then called Sondica, elderly passengers wearing berets are warmly greeted by crowds of relatives. We cut briefly to a night scene where a period steam train is entering a station where a small boy is waiting. Back in Sondica, our protagonist Pedro (played by distinguished Mexican veteran Pedro Armendáriz Jr.) is now in the terminal. He boasts a moustache, a raincoat, a jaunty red kerchief at the throat, and a whisky bottle in the fist. As we cut back to the period station (the boy embraces his father with some ambivalence, under the eyes of a Civil Guard), we hear in a sound bridge a volunteer attempt to welcome the surly Mexican. He replies that it is sad to have no one to greet you, but he first met his father in just such a situation. Pedro pointedly walks past child *txistu* (Basque flute) players in national costume playing to an appreciative crowd, only to drunkenly stumble to the ground, taking the opportunity to kiss the earth "like the Pope." Clearly, as Benet noted, by the late 1980s the nationalist project is already ripe for critique, satirized as an "operation [in] nostalgia."

We cut to a second location and a second, younger man. He is weeping gently (but only because he is chopping onions for a salad). He ignores his female partner as she tries to engage him in conversation, engrossed as he is in a tape recording of what seems to be poetry on a maritime theme, appropriate for the location in Ezeiza's native San Sebastián-Donosti. Later he contemplates family snapshots, a standard scene in the memory film. Meanwhile Pedro is now staying in a modest hotel room, making a phone call that someone fails to answer. Next leaping from a taxi to vomit in the gloomy Guipúzcoan night, he flags down the other man's car to the accompaniment of stirring strings. This second man duly takes Pedro to an address where a woman refuses to open the door. The opening sequence ends with the male couple dining together, following each one's disconnect with a female partner, initiating homosocial bonding across the generations and the continents.

Where *Brumal* staged a new feminine version of the quality period literary adaptation, *Días* recreates a modest rerun of the "symbolic" late Francoist genre set in the present and with an auteurist perspective. The brief flashbacks here, much less challenging than in, say, the Saura of previous decades, are vestigial, occurring only in the first minutes and hardly difficult to interpret (Pedro's laconic dialogue makes the identification of man and boy and the connection between the two timeframes explicit). In keeping with its title and gloomy northern setting, *Días* fails to offer, however, the aestheticized mise-en-scène typical of *Brumal* and Faulkner's "Mirovian" school. Yet in spite of this relative lack of visual pleasure, it shares elements with that corpus. There is some setting up of narrative enigmas (when asked how he got to Mexico, Pedro gruffly replies, "In a plane"). And the woman who refuses to answer the phone or the door is as yet unidentified. Apparent high-culture references, typical of the middlebrow, are teasingly opaque to a non-Basque audience. What is the origin of the poetry read on the tape? Or of the book on the desk, ominously titled *Hiltegiak* ("Abattoirs")? Where *Brumal*'s aestheticization signaled a bid for cultural capital by a novice director, *Días*'s refusal of professional polish (even the credit titles tremble in the frame) suggests rather an earnest attempt at seriousness from an established filmmaker. This artistic sobriety is in accordance with a disenchantment with the nationalist political project on whose new cultural institutions the film is nonetheless dependent. Refusing facile gratification once more, Ezeiza does not allow his audience easy nostalgia for a past that is yet more problematic for Euskadi than it is elsewhere in Spain.

When placed within the context of the Basque cultural field of the time, then, it is evident why *Días* has had little critical attention. Locals may not have warmed to the fact that Ezeiza offered the starring role to a Mexican who brings a prestigious name, lineage, and accent that nonetheless mean little in a Basque context. It is also no surprise that foreign Hispanists proved more friendly to *La muerte de Mikel*, which seasoned *abertzale* (radical independent) politics with gay thematics (however problematic), or *Vacas*, which treated Basque history with the kind of complex narrative disruptions that cry out for academic commentary. Both of these better-known films, which are regularly taught in the United States and Britain, served more easily to mark the territory and establish the authority of "Spanish film studies" in an Anglophone university institution. Ironically, however, in spite of its references back to the 1970s memory film, *Días de humo*, in its transatlantic dimension, anticipated the "transnational frame" that for Benet characterized the Spanish cinema that came after the long establishment of modernity (425).

Like *Días de humo*, Juan Sebastián Bollaín's *Las dos orillas* ("The Two Banks," 1987) is a narrative of an exile's return, although this time it is to sunny Seville rather than gloomy Guipúzcoa. And after the obligatory reference to funding from the Ministry of Culture, credit goes to the Junta of Andalucía and town hall of Seville. Surprisingly, the first shots of the film are taken from the famous "Lie to me" sequence in Nicholas Ray's *Johnny Guitar*. A fierce Joan Crawford repeats the promise of undying love fed her by a drunken Sterling Hayden (the scene is of course dubbed into Spanish). We cut to a cluttered room where a solitary Simón (José Luis Gómez) smokes, drinks coffee, and, in an instant reprise, speaks Hayden's lines himself. Called to what turns out to be the deck of a ship by his young son, he pilots the pair up the Guadalquivir somewhat incongruously to the sound of Peggy Lee's plaintive theme song from Ray's western. He moors the emblematically named and whimsically decorated *Terranova* picturesquely and implausibly alongside the Torre del Oro, which is of course one of Seville's best known tourist landmarks. Exclaiming "We're home," Simón goes on to point out the eponymous two banks of the great river: Triana and Seville itself.

We cut to a family sitting in bourgeois ennui, served by a uniformed maid and on fine china. Simón comes to the door and is recognized only belatedly by the tearful maid after his twenty year absence. His brother and sister-in-law prove more reserved, commenting pointedly on his son's alien variety of Spanish (the mother from whom Simón is separated was Latin American and they have long lived abroad). The next location is a surprisingly scenic cemetery, where Simón weeps with his brother over their parents' grave and refuses to discuss his inheritance. Later that night, father and son, in an extended still shot, advance jokily down a narrow street ("It's just like Cuernavaca!"), the scene ending with a postcard-pretty shot once more of the Torre del Oro, now handsomely illuminated. At some point after this the son invites his cousin, a luminous Icíar Bollaín (niece of the director), to explore his boat-home, making her a gift of a picture of the MGM lion logo that transforms magically into a picture of his own face. Here again we have the stress on linguistic difference in the dialogue: the boy uses the Mexican "piso" for "floor," the girl the Castilian "planta."

What this opening sequence shows us, then, is that the two banks or shores of the title are at once local, global, and ideological, referring in turn to the differences between Triana and Seville, Europe and America, and the progressive modernity of Simón versus the oppressive traditions of the family he has, in all senses, left behind. Where one embraces motion, the other clings to stasis: Simón's stolid brother claims, against the evidence of the former's nomadic lifestyle, that "a boat is for sailing and a house is for living." Simón reacts with some resistance to the suggestion that his child should attend school (interestingly, the child heroine of *Brumal* has also missed out on formal schooling).

It is striking, however, that these conflicts are somewhat muted. In spite of two decades in America, Simón bonds with his brother at the cemetery; and although they have only just met, his son and niece play happily together on the boat. While Simón's progressive beliefs are clearly at odds with those of his relations, these are hardly the two Spains of the past, locked at loggerheads. The modest tone of *Las dos riberas*, then, is not just a sign of the middlebrow or a bid for discreet artistic distinction; it is also a gesture toward the normalization and modernization of Spain after the Transition on which Benet laid such emphasis. Moreover, the film can afford to assimilate through its casting the prestige of earlier, more disturbing precedents for the Mirovian middlebrow: the *tremendista* (via José Luis Gómez, protagonist of Franco's harrowing *Pascual Duarte* [1976]) and the symbolic (via Icíar Bollaín, child star of Erice's enigmatic *El sur* ["The South," 1983]).

A vital part of Simón's *progre* (politically progressive) credentials and the film's claim to quality is cinephilia. Nicholas Ray stands here for a specifically Spanish assimilation of Hollywood auteurs: a book on the *maudit* director coauthored by none other than Víctor Erice had appeared with the Filmoteca Española in 1986, just one year before the release of Bollaín's film. The loving focus in the opening shots on the projector and celluloid and the prominent use of Peggy Lee's theme song over the credits also signal a certain cosmopolitan connoisseurship in film culture. Bollaín, an untried filmmaker much like Andreu, thus attempts (with his intended audience) to take a shortcut to artistic distinction by citing the *Johnny Guitar* scene.

What strikes the modern spectator, however, is of course that the same sequence also appears at the start of Almodóvar's *Mujeres al borde de un ataque de nervios* ("Women on the Verge of a Nervous Breakdown"), released the following year. And here we can return to Faulkner's distinction between two types of "fusion of intertexts" and, perhaps, Benet's two "layers" in Spain's (post)modern condition. In Bollaín, as in Trueba's *Ópera prima*, the reference (apparently incongruous in this markedly localist Andalusian setting) is smoothly integrated into the main plot: just as Joan Crawford's Vienna has long been separated from her beloved Johnny, so Simón has spent years apart from his wife. In Almodóvar, the fact that the two Hollywood actors are being dubbed by the separated couple, played by Carmen Maura and Fernando Guillén, would also appear to integrate the intertext into the main body of *Mujeres*'s narrative.

But the Ray citation is juxtaposed with diverse and jarring elements (it is preceded by a black-and-white fantasy sequence) and has a melodramatic effect (Maura's Pepa falls to the ground unconscious). After viewing the scene twice (as in Almodóvar once more) Gómez's Simón simply contemplates his cinematic collection with quiet pride, the very image of the cultured cinephile. Ironically, however, the heritage of Nicholas Ray, a filmmaker whose works are highly colored in all senses of the phrase, is reproduced more faithfully by Almodóvar than Bollaín, even though the "Lie to me" scene is placed in *Mujeres* in jarring juxtaposition with other heightened and extravagant filmic elements. It is a technique that harks back not just to the radical collages of *Pepi, Luci, Bom* but to the historical avant-garde, which Benet takes as ending with Almodóvar.

We remember that, as in so many heritage films, it is precisely the question of family inheritance that will be at stake in *Las dos orillas*. The same theme is prominent in our last feature to be considered here (the first to be released), Juan Caño Arecha's *Caso cerrado* ("Case Closed") of 1985, coscripted by the director with Gonzalo Goicoechea, to whom I will return later. Here the credits are held over a still shot of a home-movie camera, a fetishization of the filmmaking apparatus we also saw at the start of *Las dos orillas*. The titles themselves begin with the names of the cast, thus showing their prominence in the project: first come the newly named Pepa Flores as Isabel (fresh from her brief appearance in *Bodas de sangre*) and Patxi Bisquert as César (best known for the title role in the also recent Basque period drama *Tasio* [Montxo Armendáriz, 1984]). It is perhaps testimony to the former's continuing celebrity that the apparently uncommercial *Caso* attracted an audience that, while hardly huge, remains considerably bigger than others in our corpus: 182,000.

As Caño's camera pans over windswept hills, three women come weeping into shot. The man with the home-movie camera joins them and begins scattering ashes into the wind. We cut to the car in which Marisol's character arrives. Reverse angles establish an as-yet-unexplained conflict between her and the group. The wordless sequence (set to a "modern" 1980s electronic score) ends with an extended close up of Marisol, which then dissolves (in an editing technique that conventionally signals a flashback) to extreme close-ups of richly embroidered and jeweled fabric worn by Marisol once more. The occasion turns out to be a lavish Jewish wedding, held in the open air. In a mix of Hebrew and Castilian the rabbi unites the couple (Bisquert's character here, but not elsewhere, wears a *kippa*) and praises the groom as a focus of pride for "the community." César, he says, is at once a successful banker and a "rebel." This contradictory identity corresponds to a mix of genres that the film itself will try with some difficulty to pull off. Meanwhile, the somewhat skeptical reaction shots of some family members in the congregation are enough to make us question the happiness of the new union.

Caso cerrado thus engages us (like the other films in our corpus) with a modest enigma at the start (who is the deceased and how did s/he die?); and, as a moderate memory picture, it flashes back like *Días de humo* to a time before the narrative present. The technique is typically unchallenging, however, as the dissolve held on Marisol's face links the two time periods with no possibility of confusion. This initial temporal mode of ancient ceremony (a pagan funeral, a religious wedding) soon gives way, however, to the more urgent concerns of the present. The newlyweds may show snapshots of their honeymoon to César's mother (as we have seen, this is a leitmotif of films in this period); but in the following scene we cut to the son, severely suited in his office, discussing possible fraud at the bank. Next, more casually dressed, he is prominent in documentary shots taken from a key political campaign of the period, a demonstration against compulsory military service. Once more the fetishization of cinematic apparatus is clear here: in a leisurely sequence= shot César defends his position as a conscientious objector to a camera crew. Meeting his wife later at the bookshop that she runs, he is confronted by an official letter offering him the last chance to join up. When he repeats his refusal, Caño gives us simple shot/reverse shots that show the couple's mixed concern and affection for one another in this fraught moment.

The first fifteen minutes of *Caso cerrado* are perhaps the least artistically distinguished of the four films treated here. Apart from the lushly exotic costuming of the wedding (surely unlikely in 1980s Madrid), cinematic resources (soundtrack, camerawork, mise-en-scène, and editing) are wholly conventional. It is at the level of casting (Faulkner's fifth technique) that the film's interest lies. The renamed Pepa Flores is, as we saw in the case of *Bodas de sangre*, now identified with a Leftist militancy somewhat at odds with the bourgeois setting of *Caso cerrado* (although some viewers might bring to the opening sequence incongruous memories of a later commercial picture, *Las cuatro bodas de Marisol*). Patxi Bisquert, moreover, was well known as an ex-ETA militant who made his debut in the politically charged feature *La fuga de Segovia* ("Escape from Segovia," Imanol Uribe, 1984). The disguised Basque connection here is thus in tune with the references to other key political issues of the time, such as economic corruption and the campaign against the *mili* (compulsory military service). And it is clearest in the career of Benet's coscreenwriter. Gonzalo Goicoechea was known uniquely for his collaboration with Eloy de la Iglesia's gay- and drug-themed youth dramas of the Transition, a cycle that was just coming to a close (*El diputado* ["The Deputy"] had been from 1979, *El pico* ["The Fix"] was in 1983). *Caso cerrado*, then, a chicly dressed and comfortably furnished entrant in the quality cinema school, has clear links nonetheless to the popular and polemical *quinqui* genre, which, we remember, Benet identified as part of the second, contestatory "layer" in Spain's long settling of modernity. Indeed a familiar nonprofessional actor of such films, José Luis Fernández, nicknamed El Pirri, makes an appearance here.

In his obituary of Goicoechea in 2009, Diego Galán fails to mention *Caso*. But although he rehearses the critical attacks on de la Iglesia (appealing to the inevitable adjective "panfletario" or "propagandistic"), he rehabilitates his films by citing their appeal to a new audience (the youth in "neighborhood cinemas") and subject matter (their "witnessing" to "social themes") (Galán 2009). The blandness of *Caso*, noticeable when compared to de la Iglesia's politically engaged and sexually explicit melodramas (as highly colored in their way as early Almodóvar), thus signals an attempt to achieve a fine balance between the critically despised *quinqui* corpus of rapidly shot agitprop and the new Mirovian school of professional production values and ideological moderation.

Here the Jewish theme is vital. Like the "good homosexuals" of *El diputado* and *El pico* (characters as worthy as they are dull), Bisquert's César is an irreproachably good Jew, as moral in the economic sphere as he in his ethically based politics. Indeed the fact that Caño and Goicoechea feel no need to defend or explain the choice of a Jewish milieu that is exceptionally rare in Spanish cinema in any period signals once more that "settling" of modernity and "bringing into line" of Spain with other developed nations is Benet's great theme in this period. Like Trueba's accommodating liberated women and de la Iglesia's good gays, Caño's obliging Jews serve at once to mediate social change and to chart the shift from a cinema of memory to one focused on a more urgent and yet more problematic present.

One Tentative Conclusion

In this chapter I have addressed only the first fifteen minutes of each of my four films of the 80s. However this restricted focus can be justified in a number of ways. For example, the opening sequences of these features serve both as calling cards for little known directors anxious to establish their professional status and as frames of legibility for audiences tempted to watch those features in theatres or on television. My limited focus has also allowed for close analysis of technique, an aspect of film studies practiced by Faulkner but not Benet, in spite of the rich trove of screen caps he reproduces in his history.

As we have seen, the cinematic style of these four films is rather similar and conventional in its cinematography and editing. It observes the norms of continuity editing (e.g. shot/reverse shot, eyeline match) while indulging, again unexceptionally, in an average shot length, typical of the European films, that is rather more extended than that of the quicker-cut Hollywood movies with whom the Spanish features were (unsuccessfully, as it proved) competing in the Spanish marketplace. Interestingly, the film with the most avant-garde technique is also the most commercial: *Caso cerrado* employs some lengthy takes in unbroken sequence shots often associated with the art or auteur film, although also employed by *quinqui* exploitation director Eloy de la Iglesia, habitual collaborator of *Caso*'s coscreenwriter. In all four films, however, elements of mise-en-scène (especially costume) are carefully crafted, even if *Brumal* is the only picture requiring period art design and the only literary adaptation (a setting and a genre typical of its decade). While all of the films deal with multiple moments in time, indulging to greater or lesser extent in the memory or family history themes also characteristic of the 1980s, none of them employ the radically disruptive or challenging recreations of this temporal slippage familiar from films of the 1970s.

Highly crafted but not challenging in technique, then, our four features coincide as middlebrow in artistic terms. They also have in common their conditions of production and reception. All take advantage of new public funding schemes typical of the period, whether central (from Madrid), regional (from the Basque Country or Andalusia), or in coproduction with TVE. And if they have similar subject matter, with three treating the arrival of family members in a new town (or their return to an old town), then this may well be because, as Benet reminds us (2012, 398), state subsidies involve choices that are not just political but also artistic and even thematic. Our films would also seem to be united in their mode of consumption, or, to put it more bluntly, in their failure to attract either popular interest or critical acclaim. In this they represent the huge majority of cinema in a period when, even after the collapse in popular genres effected by the Mirovian regime, Spain was still making over one hundred films a year. Yet it is important to remind ourselves, as Faulkner does (2013, 162), that some of the films of that school, now criticized for their academic aestheticism and timidity, were huge box office successes in their time: *Los santos inocentes* ("The Holy Innocents," Mario Camus, 1984), not so different in tone or style from our corpus, was the biggest hit of its year.

What *Los santos* boasted, however, was the literary prestige that is perhaps the one condition of the middlebrow shortcut to cultural capital lacking in our corpus. The latter do make a modest bid for auteurism in that all of the directors take cowriting credits. Yet perhaps any family resemblance between them is based rather, beyond production and reception, on a certain continuity of technical and artistic personnel: two films are lensed by distinguished director of photography Alfredo Mayo and two cast the relatively untried Patxi Bisquert. It remains the case, nonetheless, that any periodization is problematic in this context. As we have seen, Faulkner and Benet differ radically in their dating and thematic focus. And while these neglected films may benefit from the former's close and sympathetic approach to the much scorned middlebrow, it is not clear how they respond to the latter's more dispersed focus. The professional production values of our films and the contemporary setting of three of them do point to the economic modernization of Spain, which is one of Benet's main themes. And our films deserve the label "postmodern" in that their political perspective is skeptical of the grand narratives of Marxism and nationalism, whether the latter is central or regional. *Caso*'s attention to Spain's small Jewish community also suggests a postmodern revision of a single story of Spanishness.

Aesthetically, however, our films do not bear out Benet's hypothesis of the postmodern as mixing and leveling or of the collapse of traditional modes of legitimation and distinction. The films' common bet on quality, easily recognizable even today, could have no meaning in such a context. Likewise, none of the films draws substantially on popular genres (*Las dos orillas* recuperates the western only in the service of practiced cinephilia). And the text of the films leaves no elements unresolved in the style of postmodern collage or, in Lyotard's term for radical and irrecuperable difference, the incommensurable.

Rather, our corpus makes recognizable reference to the past, in a way far removed from either the enigmatically "symbolic" or the brutally "tremendista" schools of the cinema of the 1970s; and, in laying the foundations for a professional audiovisual sector that combines film and television, it points forward to a more normalized future in the 1990s and beyond. Finally, then, the word that best describes this post-Transition cinema of the 1980s is perhaps, ironically enough, "transitional": artistically, industrially, and chronologically. We can now go on to see how the films of the forgotten decade compare with those of the recent present, where social and cultural factors also interact unpredictably with aesthetic or generic questions.

CHAPTER 2

Madrid de Cine
Spanish Film Screenings

Industrial Issues

The eighth edition of Madrid de Cine:Spanish Film Screenings, the major marketplace for Spanish cinema, took place on June 17–19, 2013. As ever, the event was divided into two sections: forty current features were screened for seventy-two foreign buyers from twenty-nine countries, while seventeen films that had already found distribution in foreign territories were made available to thirty-five members of the foreign press, including your correspondent. During this "junket," the press corps undertook 170 interviews with the directors and casts of the participating films.

The interviews took place in the splendid new setting of the Centro Cultural Conde Duque, which also housed the annual press conference where FAPAE (the producers' association) unveiled the new statistics on Spanish cinema performance for 2012. Other handsome new venues, apparently untouched by the crisis, were the Sala Berlanga, a publicly funded art house that staged a 3D screening of *Encierro* ("Encierro 3D: Bull Running in Pamplona"), a documentary on the San Fermín festivities in Pamplona; and Cineteca, a screen in the Matadero arts complex normally devoted to documentary that here hosted a screening of Paco León's comedy *Carmina o revienta* ("Carmina or Blow Up"). Finally, the "godfather" or *padrino* of this year's event (veteran José Coronado, featured in three films at the Screenings) presented an award to the producers of the Spanish feature with the greatest international impact in 2012. Inevitably, this went to J. A. Bayona's *Lo imposible* ("The Impossible"). (Seen by 15 million viewers in seventy countries, the English-language disaster movie was not, however, a hit in the sought-after US market.)

Illustration 2.1: Paco León, sitcom star and director of *Carmina o revienta* ("Carmina or Blow Up," 2013), at Madrid de Cine: Spanish Film Screenings

It would be fair to say that this edition of Madrid de Cine did not take place at an auspicious time. Indeed the previous weekend had proved to be the most disastrous ever for ticket sales at the Spanish box office. Yet, unlike the previous year's event where gloom was all pervasive, this time industry mavens, not normally bullish, pointed to the alleged light at the end of the tunnel. Meanwhile artistic professionals revealed in both their works and their words innovative strategies designed to deal with the unfavorable conditions that had now persisted for some years and had radically changed the supply of Spanish cinema. To anticipate my accounts of the films themselves, these new trends included postapocalyptic thrillers, literate ensemble pieces, guilty-pleasure genre pieces, unrepentant auteur movies, and technical innovators.

To return to the industry spokesmen, it was announced that in 2012 Spain had produced 182 features, thus ranking fourth in the European Union and ninth in the world. Market share at home, at an unimpressive 18 percent, was nonetheless enough to place Spain at number twenty-three in the list of fifty-seven territories studied by FAPAE. As in the previous year, more income came from foreign audiences than from the home market: a difference of 36.8 percent. Foreign viewers paying to see Spanish films in their theaters 25 million, and twenty Spanish movies grossed more than a million euros outside their home country. Ranked by territory, the highest figures earned by Spanish titles were in Mexico, Italy, the United States, France, and Argentina; and, ranked by region, in Europe, Latin America, and the United States.

Provisional numbers for 2013 seemed less reassuring. New shoots had fallen by 26 percent since the previous year (a full 50 percent over two years), and only 25 percent of these qualified as "high-budget" fiction films. Over three years the average cost of a Spanish feature had fallen by almost half, from 3 million euros to 1.8 million. Market share had, however, held steady at 17.9 percent, helped by Almodóvar's crowd-pleasing comedy *Los amantes pasajeros* ("I'm So Excited," very different to the high-flown *Los abrazos rotos* ["Broken Embraces," 2009] I discuss in the next chapter) and three genre films participating at the Screenings: *El cuerpo* ("The Body"), *Los últimos días* ("The Last Days"), and *Combustión* ("Combustion") (minority coproductions *Mama* and *Fast & Furious 6* also helped). Yet the already notorious worst-ever weekend (when box office totaled just 3 million euros) had been matched by a fall of 20 percent in cinema audiences over the previous twelve months. Box-office analysts RENTRAK blamed this result on US blockbusters, which were underperforming in Spain.

In his comments at the presentation, Pedro Pérez, respected president of FAPAE, noted Spanish cinema's mix of pride in its foreign performance and fear for its lack of connection with local audiences. He called for a campaign to bring customers back to theaters through "aggressive" cuts in ticket prices, currently inflated by a tax hike. Coronado, the *padrino*, who had just returned from Argentina and France, spoke ambivalently also of his pride in an industry that had achieved technical and artistic quality in the last fifteen years and his fear that "a country without cinema is a country without identity."

Ironically, however, foreign earning potential now counted at the preproduction stage, when funders considered investing in a project. Spanish films were thus international from the get-go. And while no statistics were available on the languages in which "Spanish" features were made, two producers had just announced films in English. The relationship between rare big-budget pictures (like *Lo imposible*) and the mass of smaller films was also fraught: Pérez hoped for a "locomotive" effect from blockbusters that promoted movie-going as an event while sheltering smaller titles in their wake.

The foreign market, savior of the Spanish cinema sector, also proved problematic. A question from a French journalist on state support for the sector elicited praise from Spaniards for his government's position on "cultural exception." But Spanish professionals also said that in Spain, unlike in France, most of the population was "prejudiced" against its home-grown cinema. Such attitudes were unjustified. Pérez claimed that you no longer heard Spanish auteurs declaring, "I make films whether the audience likes them or not."

The Mexican correspondent wondered if his continent was a "natural market" for films from Spain. Spanish producers were skeptical, noting that hostility to the Castilian accent hinders distribution in Latin America, and Spain's culture is strongly centered in Europe. They also lamented the absence of an independent theatrical circuit that left many provincial capitals without a single cinema, ironically a deficiency cited at similar professional events in Mexico.

Fantasy and Romance

In spite of combative talk, then, a sense of crisis remains ubiquitous in Spanish cinema. And it is perhaps no surprise that five years after the recession began, postapocalyptic movies were addressing this sense of intractable social change (I discuss more crisis fictions in the final chapter of this book).

First comes *Los últimos días* by tyro siblings David and Àlex Pastor. What is striking about this Barcelona-set dystopian narrative is that it begins in medias res with an inexplicable disaster already having taken place: plumes of smoke rise ominously over the avenues of the *Eixample* (the bourgeois extension of nineteenth-century Barcelona). Yet we learn in flashback that the preapocalyptic city, shot in ominous blue and gray, was hardly any better. Quim Gutiérrez plays a young techie fearing for his job when "Terminator" José Coronado is called in to fire staff at his glassily anonymous office. Gutiérrez's metro commute is alienating, his apartment building populated by sinister neighbors, and his home life soured by a reluctance to have a child with his partner (in real life Spanish demography has indeed plunged with the crisis). A missing GPS will prove to be the plot's main McGuffin: this is a generation without direction.

As an epidemic of agoraphobia gathers force, Gutiérrez and Coronado begin a buddy odyssey in search of surviving family members, tramping the empty metro tracks to discover a Sants station converted into a third-world tent city and a Hospital del Mar burned to the ground. And an impressive action sequence stages a pitched battle in a shopping mall, with piled up shopping carts serving as barricades. The moral is clear: both the welfare state and the consumer society are finished. Or in the film's own words: "The world's falling apart and we're not paying attention."

There are resonant images of decline here. Residents of Barcelona's best neighborhoods dangle pans from their windows to harvest rainwater or hang laundry to dry over their elegant stairwells. And most unusual in the film is the precision of its location in the Catalan capital. In a coda, Gutiérrez, now reunited with his pregnant girlfriend, creates a premodern rural idyll: raising indoor fruit and vegetables for a child that, spared his parents' trauma, will roam the mossy city streets, an urban jungle convincingly recreated through the film's expert effects.

It is telling that in *Los últimos días* Coronado's patriarch should die in the abandoned multiplex formerly known as Palau del Cinema (later to be the site of a real-life occupation and battle with the police by anarchist youths). And commentaries on cinema and society coincide once more in the Screenings' second postapocalyptic movie, the uncompromisingly titled *Fin* ("The End"), also by a first-time director, Jorge Torregrossa. Here one lonely survivor comments to another in what sounds like a lament for the missing Spanish movie audience: "We only exist when we're being watched."

While both films garnered a respectable domestic audience of around a quarter million, *Fin* is very different to *Los últimos días*. An ensemble piece, it tracks eight fortyish friends surprised at their reunion in a mountain cabin by a mysterious cosmic event. Bereft of cars, phones, and electricity, they roam the rocky landscape, only for each to disappear in turn. Torregrossa sets up some expert action sequences: a stampede by mountain goats and a pursuit by ravenous dogs. There is even a confrontation with a lion (*Los últimos días* stages a fight with a grizzly bear). But as the director noted in an interview, this is primarily a psychological drama, albeit one set against an apocalyptic backdrop.

Actors and screenwriters thus collaborated on a filmic version of the source novel that aimed for deeper characterization. Unlike in the original, here the apparently successful friends have lost parents and jobs and nursed grudges and crushes over twenty years. One (the excellent Daniel Grao, present at the Screenings) is secretly gay. And while the premise is (in the director's words once more) an "existential parable" for Spain's socioeconomic situation, the film responds also to its cinematic context: the rising interest in Spanish genre film, which made the project a quick sell in many foreign markets. Producer Antena 3, meanwhile, offered a substantial budget of 5 million euros to a novice director trained in the United States but appreciative of the creative control in his native country.

A slow-motion apocalypse, *Fin* also boasts some eclectic movie references, from *Picnic at Hanging Rock* to *L'Avventura* via *The Birds*. Yet the last shot, where the final couple disappear into thick mist in a sailboat, is reminiscent of the television mystery series *El barco* ("The Boat," 2011–13), also produced by private network Antena 3 (I return to *El barco* in chapter 9 of this book). As we shall see, the increasing influence of television will be a moot point in the current context of Spanish feature film.

In spite of the star presence of Maribel Verdú in *Fin* (like Coronado she appeared in three titles at the market), the film's most striking characteristic is one that is typical of TV drama: its ensemble cast. And a second pair of films at Madrid de Cine appealed to the same resource. In spite of its title, *El amor no es lo que era* ("Love Is Not What It Used to Be") is more a drama than a romantic comedy, tracing the fortunes of three couples at different stages in their lives: a young pair who hook up by accident, a middle-aged husband and wife reviving a moribund marriage, and older partners reunited after years apart. The characters' movements in space are tracked in voiceovers and graphics that use terms drawn from physics: escape velocity, parabola, and divergent trajectories. More conventionally, the three males are doctors and the three females patients. But this medical theme is, as first-time director Gabi Ochoa confirmed in interview, merely a "metaphor" for the sickness of love.

El amor begins with a shot of the AVE station in Valencia. And with the *Generalitat* (local government) one of the film's funding sources, Ochoa takes care to show attractive locations in the city. This controlled mise-en-scène is matched by restrained performances by the cast and a literate script that aims for cultural distinction. It was no surprise to learn that the director came from a theater background and had engaged in a lengthy period of rehearsal with his actors.

Ochoa's path to his first feature had not been easy. He said that the crisis had forced him to change sector (from film back to theater), pay himself less, and spend four years in preproduction. Established director Cesc Gay did not appear to have such problems with his ensemble film. Also unfortunately titled, *Una pistola en cada mano* ("A Gun in Each Hand") was funded by Catalan television and shot in Barcelona with a starry cast (like the science fiction titles, it attracted a local audience of around a quarter million). Two of the actors, Eduardo Noriega and Leonor Watling, submitted to interviews at Madrid de Cine.

Reminiscent of Ventura Pons (although shot in Castilian), *Una pistola* is made up of a series of fragments, capped by a party scene in which the protagonists coincide. Cast adrift by the decline of male role models (the title cites John Wayne), eight middle-aged men in crisis confront newly reduced circumstances: one has lost his job and lives with his mother, another tries to return to the wife he abandoned, a third is impotent, and a fourth abusive. While the dialogue seems somewhat artificial, it serves to showcase the versatility of the actors handling sensitive material and to signal serious issues within a gently comic setting.

Una pistola's signature theme of male crisis struck a chord with its creative team. The director claimed that he could afford such a luxury cast only because each actor worked for just one week on the project. And by denying them the chance to read the whole script, he enhanced their "vulnerability." Noriega noted that he is now offered fewer scripts and at an earlier (unfunded) stage of development. Spanish actors had to learn to be more proactive (he had completed a film in France) and more versatile (he had written his first script). For Gay, once more, the crisis had changed Spanish cinema's supply. With the recent rise in genre film, there were now few projects focused on "empathy for the audience." His project was thus intended to fill a gap in the market.

Genre Movies and Art Films

Madrid de Cine included two of those new genre movies, one of which was by a former auteur with a track record longer than that of Gay. Daniel Calparsoro's *Combustión* was, as noted, one of the pictures credited with maintaining Spanish cinema's market share in 2013. Yet it had also sold to thirty foreign territories. According to the director, the crisis had not affected the project, and multimedia Grupo Zeta, who had contracted him for the film, had financed it quickly. An action thriller combined with a steamy love triangle, *Combustión* replays the *Fast & Furious* franchise (whose latest episode was, as mentioned earlier, itself a Spanish minority coproduction) in a Madrid setting and with local stars Álex González and Adriana Ugarte (both present at the Screenings). The film focuses on illegal car races and suspenseful heists. If the postapocalyptic films serve as allegories of the crisis, *Combustión* might be read as a parable of the auteur Calparsoro (known for Basque-set dramas *Salto al vacío* ["Jumps into the Void," 1995] and *Asfalto* ["Asphalt," 2000]) seduced by the heady pleasures of genre filmmaking.

In an interview at Madrid de Cine, star Ugarte referred to the film with its action sequences and sex scenes as "fast food," a term she clearly used as praise. And when costar González said (like Noriega) that Spanish actors have to go abroad to work, she stated that she loved her "language and country" and would be reluctant to play "the foreign girl." But it was Calparsoro who offered the most radical comments on the current situation. When asked if he had seen a change in Spanish cinema over the course of his career, he replied that the supply was indeed changing as sources of funding changed but that the real transformation was one in leisure habits. People were no longer willing to pay for cinema tickets and movie-going was as doomed as "the Titanic." A veteran of TV series himself, he even sounded a warning on that still successful medium. Audiences for Spanish series were growing older, and soon TV fiction would hit the same barriers as cinema. Calparsoro's remedy was brutal but somewhat obscure: directors should "hide" their artistic ambitions and follow US models (albeit on a tiny fraction of Hollywood's budget). But they must keep their Spanish "soul" and "European connotation."

Given *Combustión*'s commercial shooting style, indistinguishable from a US action movie, this cultural specificity must make itself felt at the level of casting. And the Screenings' second genre piece made an argument for actors as auteurs, beyond jobbing directors. *El cuerpo* is a brutally efficient murder mystery seen by almost a million people in Spain (four times as large as any other title at the Screenings). Its high concept is easily stated: What happens when a corpse disappears from a morgue? The police investigation, headed once more by José Coronado, takes innumerable twists and turns before its shocking conclusion. Helmed by first-timer Oriol Paulo, *El cuerpo* is a vehicle for Belén Rueda, the third in a trilogy where each film was shot by a different director (the first two were J.A. Bayona's *El orfanato* [2007] and Guillem Morales's *Los ojos de Julia* [2010]). Expanding her range, Rueda, a victim in the previous titles, here plays a villainess: the manipulative middle-aged wife of younger Hugo Silva. Vital to the film's connection with local audiences is Rueda's TV history: she featured in two of Spain's longest running series, *Periodistas* and *Los Serrano*.

When asked, Rueda praised television as a "school" in which actors could develop characters over long periods. And she claimed that there were now no film or TV actors in Spain as the two media had converged. Further asked how she felt to be the "scream queen of Spanish horror," she replied that her professional role was to break taboos: crossing between TV and cinema, combining professional dramas with sitcoms, and taking her cinematic bow in a dramatic role for Amenábar (*Mar adentro* ["The Sea Inside," 2004]). Given the diversity of her career, she took pigeonholing as compliment: it meant that she had been so convincing in one role that audiences could not imagine her in another.

At a time when "la marca España" ("the Spanish brand") was much discussed in the press, it was striking that Paulo claimed that the Spanish "brand" in film was now genre movies. And Rueda took as a compliment a comment that *El cuerpo* "doesn't feel Spanish." This shift in Spanish offer from auteur to genre must pose a problem for art-movie directors who, unlike Calparsoro, are unwilling to embrace US aesthetics, yet have become accustomed to representing the nation to international audiences.

Two such traditional auteurs presented their latest works at the Screenings. José Luis Cuerda's Galicia-set period piece *Todo es silencio* ("All Is Silence") revealed a strong thematic continuity with his earlier work, especially *La lengua de las mariposas* ("Butterfly's Tongue," 1999), also adapted from a novel by Manuel Rivas. In this case the cause of repression is not, however, Francoism but rather organized crime, which evolves over twenty years from provincial smuggling to international drug trafficking. Cuerda's film poses problems to the casual viewer. Although publicity focused on box-office friendly stars (especially Miguel Angel

Silvestre, known as "El Duque" or "The Duke," from the TV role that brought him to fame), the first section of *Todo* shows the characters as children and the adults do not make an appearance until halfway through the running time. In this love triangle–cum–police investigation, the pace remains leisurely, the plot meandering, and veteran Juan Diego gives a showy turn as a criminal kingpin spouting Latin tags.

In an interview at Madrid de Cine, Cuerda claimed that it was "impossible to make cinema in Spain" and he was facing "all difficulties at once." He blamed the Spanish press for "delegitimizing" local cinema and promoting the myth that period films don't sell. Television, which he identified with the crudest kind of reality shows, was also a bogeyman: his work was more subtle and less manipulative.

Yet, in spite of this defense of art cinema, Cuerda was proud of his record as a producer, boasting that Amenábar's *Tesis* (1996) had achieved the best return on its budget in European cinema. And with its antiquarian art design and picturesque seaside locations, *Todo* is hardly as austere as the minimalist movies that dominate festivals. Moreover, it is produced by Tornasol Films, a company known for its collaboration with accessible auteurs from Ken Loach to Juan José Campanella. It would seem, then, that in an unforgiving climate, even veteran filmmakers must make artistic compromises. Indeed the theme of the film (old-school smugglers overtaken by young narcos) seems to reflect Cuerda's sense of eclipse by a more genre-friendly generation.

The second auteur film, Gracia Querejeta's *15 años y un día* ("15 Years and One Day"), had also faced production difficulties even as its leisurely pace and character-oriented script referred back to its director's earlier oeuvre. This study of a San Sebastián teenager's difficult relationship with his single mother and estranged grandfather was, like *Todo es silencio*, made by Tornasol. Bravely facing the press just days after her producer-father's death, Querejeta stressed the personal nature of the project (she was herself mother to an adolescent) but also its forced adaptation to financial circumstances (she had planned to shoot in the UK, as with her earlier *El último viaje de Robert Rylands* ["Robert Rylands' Last Journey," 1996). Echoing Cuerda, she identified lack of support from television as a "structural problem." Public TVE had no money, while private channels were limited in the kind of feature they support. Canal+, which contributed to *15 años*, had halved its screening fees. Yet even low-cost projects needed TV funding to get off the ground at a time when consumption was changing and the theatrical sector was in decline.

While *Todo es silencio* attracted a tiny audience (just sixty-one thousand), *15 años*, according to its director, started well in theaters before facing that worst-ever weekend. And, like *Todo* once more, in spite of its good taste and progressive themes (for example, a denunciation of homophobic bullying), Querejeta's film boasts audience-friendly elements, such as the ever-excellent Maribel Verdú, granted a virtuoso monologue in the final act. Unlike in a more challenging film on a similar theme (*We Need to Talk about Kevin* [Lynne Ramsay, 2011]), this testy teenager proves to have his heart in the right place.

Although, as we have seen, genre and auteur movies have evolved to meet new circumstances, my final pair of films pose a more radical challenge to the status quo. *Encierro 3D: Bull Running in Pamplona* is a documentary funded by Basque television and directed by Dutch filmmaker Olivier van der Zee. At the Screenings the director stressed the technical problems of the shoot (the use of two simultaneous cameras at ground level and cable cams for overhead shots). And although there are frequent breaks for uninspired interviews with runners (Anglo-American participants connect the film to a foreign audience), *Encierro*'s technical innovation promotes cinema as pure spectacle, beyond narrative and character.

More interesting (and the most significant film of the Screenings) is Paco León's *Carmina o revienta*. Here the innovation was in the unique mode of distribution, as *Carmina* premiered simultaneously in theaters, pay-for-view, DVD, and online streaming. At Madrid de Cine, León, perhaps the most famous TV star in Spain, claimed that this strategy was promotional, attracting for his ultra-low-budget feature the publicity it could not otherwise afford. Yet *Carmina* is also generically innovative, blurring the line between fiction and documentary (the director's mother stars as herself) and appealing to the rhetoric of the reality TV so despised by old-school auteurs. Daringly, León's sister, the accomplished actress María, also stars as a fictional version of Carmina's daughter, a gum-cracking single parent (as we shall see in chapter 6, she would also star in a similarly themed TV series). María told the press at the screening that she had learned from her amateur mother's performance what acting truly meant: not "doing" but "being there."

Although some locals were offended by regional stereotyping (the plot treats picaresque knavery in Seville), *Carmina* seasons gross humor with genuine affection for its characters and rare moments of transcendence (as when María sings a cappella at a climactic party). Sympathetic viewers may well agree with the drunken father in this sequence when he exclaims in wonder: "Life is so beautiful it almost seems real." Ironically, then, it was the coarsest comedy at Madrid de Cine that proposed not only the most intelligent way of adapting to new commercial conditions but also the most sophisticated manner of negotiating changing cinematic genres.

Thanks to Irene Ortega and Samir Mechbal at Madrid de Cine.

Note

This chapter originally appeared, in somewhat different form, as "Report on Madrid de Cine: Spanish Film Screenings," *Studies in Spanish & Latin American Cinemas* 11(1) (March 2014): 91–100.

CHAPTER 3

Almodóvar's Self-Fashioning
The Economics and Aesthetics of Post-auteurism

Art, Audience, Auteur

There seems little doubt that Almodóvar is now the most successful Spanish filmmaker of all time, whether that success is measured in terms of financial or symbolic capital. With no fewer than seventeen feature films, none of which has failed to turn a profit, and countless honors, including the Prince of Asturias Prize, the Légion d'Honneur, many Goyas and innumerable Césars, two Oscars, and an honorary Doctorate at Harvard, his career is unparalleled over more than thirty years.

Yet the contours of that career, which is of course still developing, remain unclear and cannot be reduced to the established models of film authorship associated with the "classical" auteurs (such as Welles and Rossellini) whom Almodóvar so regularly cites in his own oeuvre. Some sense of this unease comes from the diverse accounts of Almodóvar's career in different languages on Wikipedia. Thus in the English version, after rapidly dispatching "Early Life," "Beginnings," and "Short Films," the anonymous authors simply enumerate the feature films in order of their appearance (Wikipedia 2010a). The trajectory established is thus purely chronological. The French version, somewhat more analytical, adds a section on "leitmotifs" to the chronological list. Almodóvar's persistent but notably heterogeneous themes are said to be: sexual identity, parent-child relations, women, the *mise en abyme*, references to world and US cinema, drugs, and color symbolism (Wikipedia 2010b). A quote from the auteur, absent in the English version, establishes his "passion" for cinema.

Finally, spurning the simple list of films or motifs, the Spanish version places successive titles within a series of somewhat arbitrary "periods": the "experimental period" of the shorts and first two features (*Pepi, Luci, Bom* [1980] and *Laberinto de pasiones* ["Labyrinth of Passion," 1982]); the "Fellini-influenced" period, including *Entre tinieblas* ("Dark Habits," 1983) and *¿Qué he hecho yo para merecer esto?* ("What Have I Done to Deserve This?," 1984); the "maestro-influenced" period, which stretches furthest (from *Matador* [1986] to *Tacones lejanos* ["High Heels," 1991]); and the "autobiographical period," which concludes the cycle with *Todo sobre mi madre* ("All About My Mother," 1999), *La mala educación* ("Bad Education," 2004), and *Volver* (2006) (Wikipedia 2010c). In addition to this idiosyncratic periodization (apparently uncontested by Spanish-speaking collaborators of the website), the entry suggests some additional signifying contexts for the auteur, absent in other language versions, giving short sections on Almodóvar's work as a producer, on his political activities, and on his "detractors."

The three Wikipedias agree on some facts. For example, they all give Almodóvar's year of birth as 1949, although the press book for *Los abrazos rotos* ("Broken Embraces," 2009) suggests with flattering vagueness that it falls within "the 1950s" (El Deseo 2009, unpaginated). But the different versions disagree on other matters. For example the Spaniards do not mention Almodóvar's alleged sexual orientation. The French claim he is "homosexual," without offering a corroborative reference. And the Anglos call the director "openly gay," although the only link they give in the entry is to a *Time* story of 2005 in which Almodóvar himself angrily rejects the label "gay director" and is rejected in turn by the gay rights organizations who say he "has never supported" them (Farouky 2005).

My point here is not to call attention to the controversy over even basic facts, intractable as they may seem, but to suggest the difficulty in providing plausible narratives to define this matrix figure and his growing oeuvre. Specialist scholars also struggle to constrain proliferating Pedros. An international conference held at the University of Castilla-La Mancha (whose final session was attended by Almodóvar and a retinue of *chicas*) comprised four days devoted in turn to "History and Film," "Ethics and Aesthetics," "The Cinematic Universe" (on film form), and "Society, Culture, and Gender"(Zurián et al. 2005). Another volume is divided into the three broad sections of "Deconstructive Biography," "Films and Career Development," and "Gender, Art and Commerce, Society" (D'Lugo and Vernon 2013). But a third collection had employed a very different structuring principle, with loosely defined groupings of essays on "Forms and Figures" (sound, violence, comedy), "Melodrama and its Discontents," "The Limits of Representation" (girls, brothers, and nostalgia), and (finally) "The Auteur in Context" (Epps & Kakoudaki 2009). Typically here, however, Almodóvar himself has the last word, with his "diary" of the shoot of *Volver* (already posted on his website) reproduced in print as a final chapter. D'Lugo's earlier monograph had also ended with an autobiographical text, in this case a "self-interview" on *La mala educación* (2006, 145–52).

In my own research I have explored Almodóvar's unpublished short stories of the 1970s, suggesting that the key themes they share with the subsequent films (most especially the twin motifs of the glamorous and vengeful transvestite and the mature fantasizing housewife) tend to support a traditional auteurist argument based on aesthetic criteria (Smith 2009b). Almodóvar's work in text as on celluloid thus reveals a remarkable consistency of value, conceptual coherence, and stylistic unity. But I have also examined the corporate mentality of El Deseo in its commercial context, revealing how the production company seeks to preserve and promote the "figure" of Almodóvar as part of its continuing business mission (Smith 2009c, 18–20). Kathleen Vernon (2007) has noted a similar blurring of boundaries in Almodóvar's appeal to music: the songs branded as "his" when released on CD are neither written nor performed by the director, nor are they, in some cases, even featured in his films. Yet they are somehow enlisted into his ongoing creative and commercial project. The line between the artistic and the industrial is thus difficult indeed to draw.

That line is of course complicated by Almodóvar's own continuing self-commentary, which follows a double movement of revelation and concealment. D'Lugo has noted that "through the evolution of a style and a conception of filmmaking, he has moved to a critique of his own past and the culture out of which his cinema has taken shape" (D'Lugo 2006, 129). But Almodóvar's extended printed comments in the lavish press kits that have long accompanied the releases of his features seek to influence the future also, providing a template for critical interpretation.

Thus *Los abrazos rotos*'s press book (El Deseo 2009), distributed at the Cannes Festival, is divided into a number of sections: "The Title" describes the film's inspiration in Rossellini; "The Credits" reveals the "ghostly, mysterious quality" of the shoot; "Editing" suggests "the fragility of film"; "Making of" focuses on the "secrets of the people … coordinating the fiction"; "Duplication" suggests the double as a theme in the film (as shown, for example, by the two names of its main character: Mateo Blanco and Harry Caine); "Girls and Suitcases" describes the film-within-the-film, freely based on *Mujeres al borde*; "Noir" claims Penélope Cruz's Lena as a femme fatale; "Up and Down" identifies the staircase (down which

Illustration 3.1: Promotional image for Pedro Almodóvar's *Los abrazos rotos* ("Broken Embraces," 2009)

Lena will fall) as a "cinematic icon"; "The Photo" presents another inspiration for the film: a picture of lovers embracing on the black sand of Lanzarote; "Parents and Children: The Monologue" introduces a comic short that is the "child" of the feature; and finally "Declaration of Love" asserts Almodóvar's dedication to cinema, which is "not only a profession, but also an irrational passion."

Offering his own list of signifying contexts, Almodóvar thus calls attention to aspects of film technique that are generally hidden or unrecognized; to cinematic sources that his audience may have some trouble identifying; to inspirations for his plot and structuring principles of his narrative; to items of the mise-en-scène; to peripheral works spun off from the main film; and to the cinematic obsession, at once personal and professional, which, he claims, contains and explains all these diverse elements.

In this third chapter I argue that *Los abrazos rotos*, a film about a filmmaker and his craft, can be read in part as a kind of deconstructive autobiography of Almodóvar's personal and professional career to date, complex and conflicted as it is. But it is not just the range, depth, and international profile of this career that makes the Almodóvar phenomenon so difficult to address in all its aspects. It is also the changes in broader cultural spheres, which this volume seeks to address and which have, in turn, transformed the context in which Almodóvar's cinema is both produced and received. These changes, which are at once transnational and specific to Spain, deserve proper analysis before we return to *Los abrazos rotos*, which, I will argue, can be read in part as a series of reflections on current conditions for industry and authorship.

El País's business section had reported back in 2007 that government policy intended to solve Spain's growing balance of payments deficit by promoting new priorities in exports: high-tech goods and services rather than the more traditional sectors of manufacturing, textiles, and cars (Triper 2007). The sole illustration used for this article is a photograph of Almodóvar looking through a viewfinder, citing his "promotion of the Spanish audiovisual sector abroad" as exemplary of this trend in cultural exports. But in spite of such Spanish praise of Almodóvar as a key exporter, the international film sector was beset by many and varied challenges that clearly affected Spain and El Deseo. For example, the editor of *Screen International* (*SI*), the trade journal for the European film business, wrote that art house cinema was facing an "ageing problem" (Gubbins 2008). In what *SI* calls this new "post-auteurist" era, festival programmers, specialist distributors, and exhibitors now feel the lack of "bankable name directors with built-in fan bases." Moreover, younger directors favor "a more collaborative theory of production," with producers and writers "demanding more recognition of their role in the creation of a film." There has thus been a shift from "a handful of important directors" to a body of "important film-making," a change that *SI* claims to discern in the programming of recent festivals. While old-style auteurism arose in a pre-internet age when public demand was not so dominant, newer post-auteurs face the "postmodern challenge" of "engaging with audiences." Newly disrespectful, spectators may prove to be indifferent or even hostile.

This new climate of skepticism to auteurism and to film purism is compounded by trends beyond production and distribution. Thus *Sight & Sound* noted in a survey of the film industry that changes in specialized exhibition in the UK (as elsewhere) "have led to predictions that films by some of the world's finest auteurs may not make it into ... cinemas" (Patterson 2008, 30). In the same year and in a special issue, the editor of *Sight & Sound* asked "Who needs critics?" (October 2008). Given the decline in the status of film journalists, who had suffered mass culls in the United States, critics have been reduced to the status of consumer guides. Finding themselves unable to argue passionately in favor of art film or against blockbusters, because of the commercial priorities of their employers, film critics now tend to take refuge in humorous "satire" rather than to engage seriously with their chosen subject (James 2008, 17).

While perhaps only one critic in the UK still has the power to make or break a specialist release (the contributor to the *Guardian*, a national daily), film reviewers generally have rapidly "declined in market value" (James 2008, 17). Conversely bloggers, who are free from print media's sense of professional responsibility and unfettered by policy interventions from superiors (James 2008, 18), can afford to take up passionately held positions but have little social impact. A little later we will compare this Anglo-American panorama with the situation in Spain, whose media have also changed in ways discomfiting to a mature auteur like Almodóvar.

Even as the fortunes of the Spanish film industry revived (box office and market share rose in the domestic market at the end of the first decade of the millennium), old-school auteurism was under attack from two sides, at once discursive and economic: the decline in respect for art movies and the rise in status of genre films. It was a trend confirmed by the 2010 Goya Awards, where prison-set action movie *Cell 211* swept the boards and Almodóvar went home empty-handed. This was in marked contrast to previous years. As recently as 2007 an austere art movie like *La soledad* ("Solitary Fragments," Jaime Rosales) could triumph over expert but populist genre fare such as *El orfanato* ("The Orphanage," J.A. Bayona). It was significant that *SI*'s territory guide to Spain for the same year, which claimed that "Spanish films are experiencing an upturn in popularity," included a survey of distribution and box office entitled "Giving the Audience What They Want" (Evans 2010, 40).

Significantly, this apparent shift in taste also affects the distribution of Spanish films abroad. Charles Gant uses box office statistics to disprove the commonly held notion that "art house audiences don't care for [foreign language] genre films," citing a UK distributor who acknowledges the "precedent" of Spain in this crossover niche (Gant 2009). Indeed, of the ten highest-grossing European horror movies in the UK, no fewer than four (including the top two) are Spanish: *El laberinto del fauno* ("Pan's Labyrinth," Guillermo del Toro, 2006), *El orfanato*, *El espinazo del diablo* ("The Devil's Backbone, Guillermo del Toro, 2001), and zombie movie *[Rec]* (2007).

Núria Triana-Toribio offers valuable insight into this increasing convergence of art house and mainstream in Spanish cinema at home and abroad. In a major article she traces the career of two "directores mediáticos" (Álex de la Iglesia and Isabel Coixet), media-savvy cineastes who combine auteurism and commerce. As Triana writes, while Spanish film professionals have long lamented the absence of effective promotion in their cinema (Triana-Toribio 2008, 260), US film scholars such as Timothy Corrigan suggested equally long ago that the auteur is "a commercial strategy for organizing audience reception, ... a critical concept bound to distribution and marketing aims" (Triana-Toribio 2008, 261). Triana relates the rise of the *mediáticos* in Spain to increasing pressure on distribution: the saturation of screens requires aspiring auteurs to compete as never before to "place their product" (Triana-Toribio 2008, 262).

Triana also studies in detail the new auteurs' homepages. Hosted by a site run by transnational retailer FNAC, they both present themselves as "potentially authentic and autonomous modes of expression" (Triana-Toribio 2008, 263). In practice, however, the self-authored websites negotiate that curious combination of personal intimacy and physical distance characteristic of the web, creating "auteur personas" with distinct (and distinctive) "habitus": a Bourdieu-originated term defined here as "schemes of perception, thought, appreciation, and action" (Triana-Toribio 2008, 272). Both sets of habitus in these case studies are contradictory. De la Iglesia ostentatiously divests himself of expertise in any area except gastronomy, even as he presents himself as a "pure filmmaker" in thrall to obsessive cinematic creation (Triana-Toribio 2008, 271, 273); Coixet portrays herself as an engaged and educated artist, citing Gramsci and Stendhal, even as she proudly displays her work as a director of TV commercials and provides links for consumers to buy her products (Triana-Toribio 2008, 273, 275).

Both De la Iglesia and Coixet have had features produced by El Deseo. And Triana had earlier dedicated a study to the Almodóvar brothers' production company, a Spanish pioneer in promotion and marketing (2007). In this piece she examines a question that is also found in the specialist trade press: transnationalism. And Triana seeks to link the increasing academic interest in the topic with the industrial changes recounted by the trade press. She reminds us, however, that El Deseo "boasts a world-wide projection already well established long before we started to hear the word 'transnational' in film studies" (Triana-Toribio 2007, 156).

In Triana's account the company was first founded to take advantage of the Sociality government's institution of advance subsidies in the 1980s, described as "a new form of financing films through a partnership with the state" (Triana-Toribio 2007, 156). However, El Deseo's aim from the start, benefiting from Agustín Almodóvar's business acumen and activism, was to "use national financial resources [to] make Spanish cinema take pride of place among the world cinemas in a sustained manner" (Triana-Toribio 2007, 157). (We saw in the previous chapter that Agustín is himself well aware of this policy.)

Triana cites instead Esther García, the company's head of production, who notes that, unlike other Spanish producers, El Deseo has a strong record of overcoming the problem of international sales. Moreover, the company has both opted for "quality" and kept budgets low (around 2 million euros). Triana wonders whether such a phenomenon deserves a new name. Surely the cinematically literate "transnational" audience for Almodóvar's films, however actively cultivated, is little different to the old-school cinephile public who sought out foreign-language films abroad? She concludes that while "the strategies for making films that travel [may] have changed ... the films that travel are little different from the past" (Triana-Toribio 2007, 159).

Going further in this revisionist line, she enumerates a series of highly localist linguistic and cultural factors that suggest that *Volver*, say, is firmly "grounded in [its] nation of origin" (Triana-Toribio 2007, 160). Movies with larger budgets, which are also made to be consumed internationally (such as del Toro's *El laberinto del fauno*), may, paradoxically, prove more vulnerable in the future, as they are funded only reluctantly by TV companies who are obliged by Spanish law to invest

5 percent of their income in cinema. Unfortunately the Spanish audience has "turned its back on [the small budget] home production" that comprises the great majority of local feature films (Triana-Toribio 2007, 161).

Triana's media-savvy directors are, she says, "middle brow"; and the elastic nature of El Deseo's definition of "quality" (which extends even to genre films that push the envelope of conventional expectations) also seems to conform to Bourdieu's understanding of the middlebrow as that which offers insecure audiences a shortcut to cultural capital that must elsewhere be laboriously acquired. Indeed if we return to Bourdieu's classic study *Distinction: A Social Critique of the Judgement of Taste,* we find a telling example of ethics and aesthetics in cinema. When confronted with a photograph of an old woman's gnarled hands, elite informants invoke art film in their responses, saying the subject could "almost be a character" out of Bergman, Dreyer, or Welles; likewise a chiaroscuro shot of a gasworks at night is said to be "beautiful because of [its] contrasts" (Bourdieu 1996, 45–46).

In a similar way, Almodóvar's own citations of auteur cinema, increasingly prominent in later films, serve to establish his own cultural capital and to aestheticize his subjects. But note that, unlike in the cases of Bourdieu's photographs, which are studiously unpleasurable before they undergo the process of elite interpretation, Almodóvar's cinema, extravagantly art directed and colored, requires little cultural expertise to appreciate aesthetically. Indeed his films, less severe than many other auteurs past or present, have been regularly attacked for their visual excesses. Perilously poised between high art and vulgar commerce, Almodóvar's own oeuvre may thus well merit the label of middlebrow, a term discussed at length in the first chapter of this book. Bearing this tricky position in mind, we can now turn in the remainder of this chapter to examine how Almodóvar's self-fashioning can be re-read in the various contexts sketched out above at the crucial time of the production and release of *Los abrazos rotos,* his seventeenth feature.

Autobiography and Industry

First of all, *Los abrazos rotos* clearly takes up its place in the late "autobiographical period" identified by the Spanish Wikipedia page, focusing as it does on a middle-aged filmmaker (Mateo Blanco, played by stage veteran Lluís Homar) who serves as a stand-in for Almodóvar himself during a time when the director was approaching his sixtieth birthday. Mateo's supposed lost masterpiece, reassembled only at the end of the film, is (as the press book informed us) called *Chicas y maletas* ("Girls and Suitcases") and is a clone of Almodóvar's international crossover success *Mujeres al borde* of more than twenty years earlier.

Confessional, albeit in a symbolic mode, such self-reference attempts to render long-term fans complicit with the film' creator by evoking shared and fond memories of past cinematic pleasures. In this case, however, Almodóvar does not engage the richly particularized cultural location of *Volver*. *Los abrazos rotos*'s background, both historical (the film is set in 1992 and the present) and geographical (the film was shot in Madrid and the Canaries), is only lightly sketched in. The film is of course a coproduction, but this time not with France (Ciby 2000 and Pathé were long term partners); instead, it was produced with funding from the United States (in this case the major Universal's recently revived international arm). And as has been the case at least since *La flor de mi secreto* ("The Flower of My Secret," 1995), the budget was covered in advance by foreign presales.

Clearly unconcerned in this transnational project by current social conditions in contemporary Spain, Almodóvar went further in his personalized projection. In repeated interviews he assured readers that Blanco's blindness (here caused by a car accident) was related to the director's own recently acquired "photophobia," a sensitivity to light that resulted in severe migraines (see Smith 2009a, 20). Mateo's conflict with the malign magnate who is the producer of his film (Ernesto Martel, played by film veteran José Luis Gómez) also recalls Almodóvar's early struggles with moneymen before the founding of El Deseo gave him artistic independence. For example, he once said in an interview that he was obliged against his wishes to cast his producer's partner in the lead female role in *Dark Habits* (1983) (Vidal 1989, 94–95). In *Los abrazos rotos*, Cruz's Lena is also the lover of producer Martel, on whom both star and director depend. While such conflicts may not correspond to Almodóvar's current situation (in which his loyal brother is his sole producer), this theme does connect with the current trend elsewhere for producers to seek more credit for their creative contribution. Moreover, the stress on movie finance in *Los abrazos rotos* (Cruz's character cannot leave the wealthy, abusive partner who is funding Mateo's film) testifies obliquely to the frequent and traumatic changes in film funding in post-Franco Spain.

Interestingly, in Almodóvar's two previous projects with cineaste protagonists (*La ley del deseo* ["The Law of Desire," 1988] and *Bad Education*), the main characters were gay men enamored of younger lovers. Although Homar (born 1957) is presented in *Los abrazos rotos* as the perfect heterosexual partner for the still youthful Penélope Cruz (born 1974), in *La mala educación* the same actor had played an aging pedophile whose obsession with the handsome Gael García Bernal (born 1978) was depicted as poignant, if not pathetic. Almodóvar stresses in *Los abrazos rotos* the continued sexual desirability of a mature protagonist (the film begins with Mateo somewhat implausibly picking up an attractive young woman on the street). But he also suggests the same indifference to sexual orientation that is characteristic of his own media projection. Displacing queer interest onto the minor character of Martel's son (also sexually obsessed with Mateo), Almodóvar blurs that conflict over his own sexuality that has been played out in press coverage in different countries and languages. The film's plot thus serves as a distorting mirror for the real-life concerns of a continuing media metanarrative.

Beyond disguised autobiography, Almodóvar also makes a clear bid in *Los abrazos rotos* for the traditionalist criteria of auteurism, albeit without neglecting overt visual pleasure: the production values remain reassuringly high (especially the expert art design by Antxon Gómez); the themes of artistic creativity and *amour fou* run through the entire oeuvre (although the crazed lovers in *La ley* and *La mala educación* are not the film-obsessed directors but the young boyfriend played by Antonio Banderas and the aging ex-priest played by Homar, respectively); and the stylistic signature is unmistakable, even given the presence of a new and potentially disruptive director of photography (Rodrigo Prieto, who lensed the hyperkinetic *Amores Perros* [Alejandro González Iñárritu, 2000]). But these artistic questions are also industrial: sold initially on the back of the "figure" of the director (the Spanish poster carried the now familiar single credit, "Un film de Almodóvar") the new feature strove to further El Deseo's continuing business mission of promoting the durable prestige of the company's only begetter.

Given his enviable track record, Almodóvar had access to the most prestigious platforms to promote a work that aspired to high-profile media coverage over an extended period of time. As early as the shoot in Lanzarote, *El País* (the only outlet given access at this stage of production) ran a lengthy and reverent set report titled "Under the Almodóvar Volcano" (Fernández Santos 2008). A more skeptical profile of Penélope Cruz by star writer Elvira Lindo served as the cover feature in the paper's weekly magazine just weeks later, ensuring that the paper's up-market readers had no opportunity to forget the new film as it went into postproduction (Lindo 2008).

El Deseo thus deployed its now traditional skills in marketing, which are held to be characteristic of those rare media businesses that spearheaded Spanish service industries at home and abroad. Yet perhaps the increasing emphasis on Cruz in the promotional campaign derived from the company's concerns about the aging of the art house and its audience and the difficulty for Spanish films to connect with a skeptical local public. In April 2009 (as the film was released) Spanish *Vanity Fair* ran a frankly risible cover feature on the star couple with the strap line "Intimate and Secret" (*Vanity Fair* 2009). Penélope's pull quote was, "Both of us know that when we are flirting we are on dangerous ground"; and Pedro's "At 40 I almost fathered a child." In the glossy spread inside, Penélope pretends to play the harp for Pedro, as he reclines languorously on a chaise longue; or, again, she poses pensively in a Chanel couture bridal gown.

However unconvincing this media marriage may be, such role-play serves somewhat narcissistically to echo and reinforce *Los abrazos rotos*'s main plot strand: the love affair between Cruz's character and the brilliant director who casts her in his film. In an age widely believed (even in the trade press) to belong to the post-auteur and in the midst of a global economic crisis felt with particular intensity in Spain, even the most bankable of veteran name directors may feel the need to lean more heavily than before on a younger celebrity, especially if she is the only Spanish actress readily recognizable abroad. Moreover, as Almodóvar's longest and highest budgeted feature, *Los abrazos rotos* seeks to separate itself from those small Spanish pictures on which local audiences had consistently turned their backs, staking its claim to the same transnational audience that prestige pictures like *El laberinto del fauno* won around the world. Whether that audience crosses over with the old-school cinephile public (as Triana believes) or not, *Los abrazos rotos* was of course conceived as a film that would not only travel but would take most of its revenue abroad.

At a corporate level, there are other signs of El Deseo's desire to connect with changing audiences. The Almodóvar brothers take their social responsibility seriously. Doing well by doing good, they see the sponsorship of younger directors, often from Latin America, as a cinematic duty that brings them little economic benefit but considerable credibility and good will. One El Deseo coproduction, Lucrecia Martel's well-received *La mujer sin cabeza* ("The Headless Woman"), was released just a few months before *Los abrazos rotos*. And responding to the pressure for disintermediation (going directly to the consumers), Almodóvar has, since *Volver*, exploited the internet in order to bypass the mainstream media in self-written blogs on two homepages to which I return later.

Also responding to the challenge of the internet and in a new strategy of deaggregation, Almodóvar separated off part of *Los abrazos rotos*'s film-within-the film in a crudely comic short satirizing the right-wing Partido Popular, *La concejal antropófoga* ("The Cannibalistic Councilor"), which was distributed independently on the web and television. Starring as it did Carmen Machi, Spain's most popular female TV star, the short can be read as an attempt to connect with the mass audience who had followed Machi for some years on Tele 5's top-rated and long-running sitcom *7 vidas* ("7 Lives," 1999–2006) and its spin-off *Aída* (2005–). The lavish photo shoots mentioned earlier might also be read in this way, as a canny (if unmonetized) deaggregation of that once-fetishized and unified work of art, the quality feature film. Moreover, when the DVD version of *Los abrazos rotos* appeared in Spain, it was as a luxury two-disc boxed edition, replete with the extras (the short film, a photo gallery, and footage of Pedro directing Penélope) that the perfectionist Almodóvar had long resisted providing for earlier releases. With characteristic reflexivity, these commercial questions are incorporated into the film itself, where the "making-of" footage shot by Martel's gay son plays a significant part in the plot.

The renewed debate between art film and genre movies, prominent in Spanish cinema of the 2000s, is also internalized in *Los abrazos rotos*, fed back into perceptions of Almodóvar's own artistic development. Mateo's production manager Judit (steely Blanca Portillo) remarks dismissively early on that Mateo might make more money by writing "one of those fantasy films for kids" (the blind director has now become a screenwriter with the pseudonym "Harry Caine," presumably named for Welles). Although this remark may well be a wry acknowledgment that teen movies, both domestic and foreign, are now the biggest grossing features in Spain, a central sequence in *Los abrazos rotos* has Mateo and his lover Lena, played by Cruz, intently watching Rossellini's *Viaggio in Italia* ("Journey to Italy," 1954) on television. But, as if aware that this allegiance to old-school auteurism may no longer be shared by his audience, Almodóvar makes sure to embrace genre film with equal warmth. Mateo's lost masterpiece *Chicas y maletas*, indulgently described as "a work of genius" by Judit in the final sequence of the film, is no Wellesian or neorealist drama but rather one of those farcical comedies that Almodóvar himself abandoned in the quest for "quality" that became so central to El Deseo's corporate mentality. There is thus an unresolved ambivalence to genre film here. When Judit's son improvises a vampire premise for a film (one that Pedro himself had orally recounted at the conference held at the University of Castilla-La Mancha, mentioned earlier), Mateo eagerly climbs on board, offering to help the young man with the script. We are thus left in no doubt that this most populist of teen-friendly themes is worthy of creative development.

The final area to consider in this survey of how *Los abrazos rotos* interacted with changing social and cultural conditions is one to which I have already briefly referred: newspapers and internet. Although El Deseo is often acclaimed for its professional marketing and Pedro has long been indefatigable in his promotional activities, it is striking that the press coverage in Spain is decidedly mixed. Almodóvar has openly argued with the Spanish Film Academy (AACCE), which has failed to nominate his features for their prizes as often as he would have liked (Anon. 2005). The premiere of *Bad Education* was marked by Almodóvar's controversial and unfounded claim that, after the terrorist outrages in Madrid on the eve of a general election, the Partido Popular were planning a coup d'état (see D'Lugo 2006, 128). Likewise, the main media story on the release of *Los abrazos rotos* was not the film itself, but Almodóvar's public quarrel with the leading newspaper, *El País*, which had featured so often within his films and had already provided so much advance publicity for his newest feature.

Almodóvar, the pioneer of Triana's media-savvy directors, had two homepages at the time. The first was hosted, like those of de la Iglesia and Coixet, by French book and video retailer FNAC (Clubcultura 2005). Although claimed as an "official site" in three languages, by 2010 it had not been updated for five years, with the most recent "News" being the preproduction of *Volver*. The biography given in the "Autor [sic]" section was skimpy, but some family photos appeared there; the "Films" section offered posters, brief synopses, and, for later works "Comments of Pedro" (i.e., self-penned texts originally from the press books) or access to dedicated sites; "Bibliography" and "Scor [sic]" allowed surfers to buy books and CDs associated with films from FNAC; while "Specials" collected links to Almodóvar's exhibition of still photography (also held at FNAC's central Madrid store) and his self-interviews. While the design of the layout was reminiscent of El Deseo's distinctive graphics (designed by Juan Gatti), the lack of attention to detail (the frequent misspellings and tardy updating) are far from Almodóvar's normal perfectionism. Moreover, with no facility for posting comments (de la Iglesia and Coixet actively participate in online forums with fans) the site remained fixated on its master's voice and declines to engage with audiences. As a commercial strategy for organizing reception, this avowedly auteurist site was clearly deficient.

Almodóvar's personal focus was now evidently elsewhere. And a second, more professionally presented trilingual site, which also claimed to be "official," hosted his more recent blog (Almodóvar 2009). This site offered texts and photos (carefully copyrighted to Pedro himself) minutely documenting the pre- and postproduction processes of *Los abrazos rotos*. Framed by stylish graphics designed to evoke the sprocket holes of a roll of celluloid, the text was in Courier typeface, evocative of a vintage typewriter and intended to personalize the electronic medium. Aware of the demand for intimacy in such a format, Almodóvar meditated on the nature of his blog in somewhat contradictory fashion. It is worth citing him at length:

> *I started writing this kind of "journey notes" in October and I intend to go on recording what is happening in my life in the little free time I have for writing. I hope to carry on doing it at least until shooting finishes. It will be a way of letting off steam for me and also provide a future memento. And above all, it will increase my level of stress and anguish, because literally I haven't even got time "to wipe my ass," as my mother would say. What's more, I'm not a diary writer. Apart from scripts (which I write because I'm driven by a hysterical need to tell stories, I need fiction like I need oxygen) I've only been able to write the rest of my literary output under pressure, in circumstances in which I never had any time. Even if it's hell on my nerves, I've decided to write this blog while I'm working, even if at times it may be rushed and arbitrary. The good thing about writing a blog is that no one can accuse you of being egocentric. ... I promise to tell only the truth, but that doesn't mean I'm going to tell you everything about me and about the film and its preparation. On the contrary, I intend to say as little as possible about the story and the characters, I'll wander around on the fringes, in purely tangential elements. You'll think I've got a real cheek, and I'm sure you're right. (Anything to celebrate the lack of intermediaries). (Almodóvar 2009)*

In spite of his tantalizing promise of disclosure, then, Almodóvar also admits that he will conceal key elements of his self and of his new film. Indeed, devoted as he claims to be to cinema, he gives away nothing at all about his private life, beyond the characteristic reference to his beloved late mother. And yet he speaks in the first person, addresses the reader directly in the second person, and celebrates the "lack of intermediaries" specific to his chosen genre and medium. This double movement of revelation and concealment is, as we have already seen, typical of Almodóvar's self-fashioning as a public artist in which carefully selected aspects of his life and art feed off one another.

Similar to the shooting diary for *Volver*, the blog provides fascinating material (both text and image) on Almodóvar's working methods: script corrections in north Africa and Mexico, table reads with the actors in Pedro's office, hair and costume tests for Penélope in El Deseo (her character will undergo the same process in the film itself), and shooting on location in Lanzarote and in the same studios at Barajas outside Madrid where *Mujeres al borde* was filmed some two decades before. However, the blog also displays a disconcerting lack of self-consciousness, revealing as it does Almodóvar's residence in luxury hotels around the world (from Tangiers to Cuernavaca) and dwelling on his participation in the annual Rose Ball in Monaco, which, in his honor, was given a *movida* theme. At a time of unprecedented economic crisis in Spain, Almodóvar documents himself consorting with the crowned heads of Europe, whom he does not fail to flatter (Princess Caroline is said to be "warm" and Prince Albert "charming"). Lacking once more a facility for comments from readers, the blog is, in spite of its disclaimer to the contrary, profoundly egocentric.

Absent from the (professionally translated) French and English versions of this second website, but given pride of place on the Castilian original, are extended texts documenting Almodóvar's latest feud with *El País*. Significantly, they turn around El Deseo's transnational projection, which, we remember, takes pride of place in the company's image of itself. Writing from Cannes, where *Los abrazos rotos* was in competition for the Palme d'Or (26 May 2009), Almodóvar inveighs against the festival coverage by *El País*'s chief film critic, Carlos Boyero, and its arts editor, Borja Hermoso, perhaps the highest profile "detractors" of the director.

How can we read this polemic in the context of Almodóvar's continuing self-fashioning? Clearly it was a self-defeating strategy for the celebrity director, in that he succeeded only in lending the critic, much less known than himself, the oxygen of publicity that he no doubt craved. And anyone reading Almodóvar's texts receives an unhealthy impression of, at worst, paranoia or, at best, "negativity bias" (Marano 2003). The latter is a widespread but unattractive psychological quirk whereby critical comments, however infrequent, are felt by their victim to outweigh positive opinions, however numerous and flattering. While one could perhaps read the polemic cynically as part of Almodóvar's continuing attempt to compete to place his product ahead of that of other auteurs, it seems more likely that, as *El País*'s staff committee observed (in an open letter posted on the paper's website [May 27, 2009]), his behavior served rather to damage his "figure," the reputation that El Deseo is so devoted to burnishing.

But beyond pragmatics (Almodóvar could hardly have devised a surer way of alienating the Spanish press), this quarrel responded to and was facilitated by broader cultural changes, mentioned earlier, with which Almodóvar appeared to be unfamiliar. Thus the journalists' collective clearly felt no need to genuflect to an Oscar-winning auteur, whom they remind in their response is "not sacred." This newfound skepticism to auteurism, within whose hallowed precincts Almodóvar was in any case never securely implanted in Spain, is combined with changes in film criticism as an institution. In an age of declining readership (*El País*'s circulation, the largest nonsporting daily in Spain, is only around 400,000), even the quality press may feel the need for controversy to boost newsstand sales and internet footfall (the polemic garnered 131,000 hits). Boyero, flagrantly solipsistic and crudely satirical, is exemplary here, in that he openly refuses to engage seriously with his chosen subject even though he writes for what is felt by many Spaniards to be the newspaper of record. In this he does indeed mark a radical break with the earlier and less subjectivist traditions of Spanish film criticism (such as that practiced by *El País*'s previous critic, Ángel Fernández Santos, nostalgically invoked by Almodóvar), which aspired to objectivity and avoided personal idiosyncrasy.

Hence, when Almodóvar attacks Boyero for walking out of a festival screening by demanding Iranian auteur Abbas Kiarostami (a piece of evidence he takes to be damning) or insists on the sanctity of the distinction between news and comment, he shows himself to be insensitive to changes in the habitus (to schemes of perception, thought, appreciation, and action) of both journalism and film culture in general, changes that younger "directores mediáticos" have proved more skilled at negotiating. The fact that Boyero is so clearly supported by *El País* as a matter of policy can only prove this point. Out of tune with the new demands on newspapers, Almodóvar also displays a tin ear for the particular pleasures and potentials of the blog, even as he reproduces the (too) passionately held positions typical of that medium. Revealing no personal intimacy, other than an acute sensitivity to criticism, and exposing the physical distance his glamorous lifestyle puts between him and his public, he can only alienate a Spanish audience already more kindly disposed to genre films than to art movies.

Media Stories

I would suggest finally, then, that these public arguments, which now constitute the principle vehicle for Almodóvar's continued self-fashioning, are more significant than they first appear. Indeed, they are structurally similar to the rise of "scandal politics," which has been treated so acutely by Catalan sociologist Manuel Castells. For Castells, political scandals (exceptionally frequent in Spain, as elsewhere) are one of the main characteristics of the new "network society": they result from the lack of clear differences in ideology between political parties; reveal that questions of personality now supersede those of policy; and demonstrate the complicity and volatility that results when figures from fields such as politics become active participants in the media, only to find themselves unable to control the resulting "stories" (Castells 1997, 337–42).

Mutatis mutandis, this is a fine description of Almodóvar's predicament. With no clear distinction now accepted between high and low culture and with Pedro's personality long used to promote his films, Almodóvar is not only actively complicit with the media, he even calls attention to that complicity, as when he cites in his blog the favor he did to *El País* in granting the paper unique access to the shoot of *Los abrazos rotos*. Yet, like the malign magnate at the heart of his film whose lover is seduced away from him even as he funds her career, Almodóvar and his devoted coworkers prove unable to control the outcome of their proliferating media strategies.

More particularly in the age of the internet, amateur "detractors," previously excluded from the mainstream media, now possess a powerful echo chamber for any negative views they may come across. Triana writes of her "mediáticos" that they "reconcile the paradoxes surrounding authorship in Spanish cinema [by] foster[ing] the cult of personality on which traditional auteurism rests while at the same time making this individuality accessible to the wider public" (2008, 276). The problem, then, for El Deseo is to devise plausible narratives that can effect a reconciliation between the (public) personality and the (private) individuality of an increasingly complex matrix figure.

To return to the starting point of this chapter, such polemics may barely compromise Almodóvar's current status as the most successful Spanish filmmaker of all time, especially outside his native country. And Marsha Kinder has shown convincingly how the conspicuous self-referencing in *Los abrazos rotos* enriches the film, demanding that spectators reread the director's "entire body of work" at a crucial time for film: "an historic moment when the medium has gone digital and its methods of distribution are being redefined" (Kinder 2010, 28, 33). The changes in broader cultural spheres that I have sketched here, both economic and aesthetic, thus render Almodóvar's position and oeuvre more precarious. Almodóvar was once known, especially in Spain, by the label "postmodern," a term suggesting a radical skepticism to authoritative forms of politics and culture in his cinema, as in his person. Ironically, however, it has been more recently, when he has openly embraced political activism (on behalf of the Socialist Party) and high culture (on behalf of the venerable auteurs he has so showily cited in his own films), that Almodóvar's own hard-won authority has been so frequently called into question. If the self-fashioning that he has pursued so doggedly can be described as a kind of deconstructive autobiography or post-auteurism, it is because of just such discursive paradoxes.

Note

This chapter originally appeared, in somewhat different form, as "Almodóvar's Self-Fashioning: The Economics and Aesthetics of Deconstructive Autobiography," in *A Companion to Pedro Almodóvar*, ed. Marvin D'Lugo and Kathleen M. Vernon (Blackwell Publishing, 2013), 21–38.

PART II

Television

CHAPTER 4

Media Migration and Cultural Proximity
A Specimen Season of Television Drama

TV Contexts

On April 13, 2009, a glamorous premiere was held at the Cine Capitol, the last surviving picture palace on Madrid's Gran Vía. Stars posed for the press photographers and TV cameras, and a horde of screaming fans blocked the traffic as they fought for a glimpse of their favorites. Surely this was a rare case of Spanish cinema connecting with the local youth audience?

In fact, what was showing on Madrid's biggest screen that night was the first episode of the third season of a television show: national network Antena 3's top-rated high-school drama *Física o química* ("Physics or Chemistry," 2008–11). It would seem that television, a notoriously domestic and everyday medium, prized for its cultural proximity to the national public, had appropriated not only the mass audience in Spain, but also the distant glamour of a star system that was once restricted to cinema. There could be no clearer example of the migration between the two media in Spain than this high profile event.

In the same month, *Fotogramas*, the main popular Spanish movie magazine, published a report called "Generación TV 2009." It featured no fewer than thirteen young actors (including four from *Física o química*) who, it claimed, had "renovated" television fiction and now had one foot in film (*Fotogramas* 2009). The magazine also reported on its own awards ceremony in which readers voted for their favorite productions and protagonists in both media.

But this new prominence of TV actors is only the most visible face of media migration. In their monumental study of producers in Spanish cinema from its beginnings to 2005, Esteve Riambau and Casimiro Torreiro refer to the period since 1995 as "the era of the audiovisual" (as opposed to "cinema"), marking as it does the definitive "convergence" between the film industry and the television companies (2008, 901). The authors state that from that date, television companies took over from film distributors as the "locomotive" of cinema production. As they describe it, the belated arrival of private television in Spain (at the beginning of the decade) signaled not only the arrival of a few foreign investors (notably Silvio Berlusconi at Tele 5) but more importantly the "alliance" of Spanish film producers with other Spanish media. The highest profile example they give is that of the celebrated veteran Andrés Vicente Gómez, who joined forces with Sogecine, itself allied with the PRISA conglomerate and Canal+ (2008, 903). Or again, if Spanish cinema producers have sometimes sought out "transnational support" with Latin American partners through coproduction scheme Ibermedia (2008, 910), they have relied more heavily on local TV companies and on national banks, such as the Instituto de Crédito Oficial and, in Catalonia, the Institut Català de Finances (2008, 911). It is striking that Tele 5, once notorious for TV trash programming, has gone on to produce some of the most artistically and commercially successful films in recent Spanish cinema, from Guillermo del Toro's *El laberinto del fauno* ("Pan's Labyrinth") and Agustín Díaz Yanes's *Alatriste* (both 2006) to Steven Soderbergh's *Che* (2008).

As Lorenzo Vilches, coordinator of OBITEL (the invaluable annual survey of TV fiction in Spain and Latin America [Vilches 2007]) has also pointed out, domestic television production has in recent years gone from strength to strength, even as cinema has seemed to be in decline (FórmulaTV.com and Cascajosa 2007). This view is certainly supported by the innovative new TV titles broadcast in Spain for the spring season 2009, which attracted a faithful viewing public. As Vilches once more points out (in a monthly survey of audiences published online by the Universitat Autònoma in Barcelona), daily viewing times rose by 5 minutes in February on the figure for 2008, reaching an all-time high of 244 minutes per person (Vilches 2009). And this came at a time when the television industry, already suffering from the general economic crisis that has hit Spain harder than any other Western European state, has also been obliged by the Ley del Cine of December 28, 2007, to make a financial transfer of 5 percent of income to the loss-making cinema sector (Ley del Cine 2007). Ironically this law also proposed (like scholars Riambau and Torreiro) that filmmaking should be understood as being integrated within a general audiovisual sector ("the whole of the audiovisual") even as it argued that the former deserved subsidies that private television does not receive.

In spite of these changed circumstances, distinctive structural elements of the Spanish TV ecology remain in place: the continued dominance of locally produced quality fiction in the evening; the late and lengthy time slots (with prime time beginning at 10 PM and dramas playing for at least an hour and a half); the extended and irregular commercial breaks (with channels now announcing to impatient audiences as they cut to commercial: "Volvemos en un minuto" ("Back in a minute") or, more frequently, "Volvemos en cinco minutos" ("Back in five minutes"); and the merciless competition between the five main national channels, which ensures that the nightly grid is subject to last-minute changes in the name of counterprogramming.

The most distinctive and durable difference between Spanish and Latin American television, however, remains in their respective programming grids. While the latter schedule daily *telenovelas* across prime time, in Spain peak viewing hours are dominated by the weekly series dramas that are locally produced. Clearly such shows, which rarely have more than twenty episodes a year (one series I study here had just nine in its first season), have much higher budgets and production values than the *telenovelas* that boast over one hundred installments and are shown in Spain, if at all, only in the daytime. Moreover, the performance style and use of incidental music remain typically more restrained in Spanish productions than in, say, Mexican. It is characteristic that in a very rare case of the Spanish recreation of a Latin American format (the ubiquitous *Yo soy Betty, la fea* ["Ugly Betty"]), the resulting show was very different from both the Colombian original and the US version (see Smith 2009d).

In spite of these continuities, there are also changes in the sector. Public Televisión Española's generalist channel (known as "La Primera"), which seemed in terminal decline, favored as it was by a diminishing, older audience that is unattractive to advertisers, fought back with new fictions that have attracted wider and younger demographics. Vilches reports (2009) that TVE-1 led the field in February for the third month running, with an average share of 17.3 percent. This is an improvement of 1.1 points over the course of the year, a significant achievement for the national public broadcaster committed to generalist programming at a time when audiences in Spain, as elsewhere, are thought to be ever more fragmented. The main private channels were forced into second and third place, with Antena 3 taking 15.3 percent and Tele 5 (in earlier years the clear leader with innovative programming in both fiction and reality shows) reduced to just 14.9 percent.

New forms of distribution have also made current Spanish TV fiction more easily available to foreign as well as domestic viewers. TVE's "A la carta" web service (Televisión Española 2009), trialed in 2008, is (unlike the BBC's equivalent) generally accessible to surfers abroad, as are similar services on the private channels' websites. ("A la carta" also offers streaming access to a substantial range of TVE's back catalogue of classic shows.) Within hours of their first broadcast, substantial portions of new titles have also been placed by fans on YouTube. And TV movies, making a major comeback in Spain, especially on Antena 3, are available on DVD days after transmission. TV fiction has thus begun to rival film not just in production values and artistic ambition but also in international reach and durability.

In recent years the only substantial change to fiction formats has been the emergence of the new genre of sketch comedy, pioneered by Tele 5. *Cámera café* ("Coffee Cam"), a minimalist office farce shot from the supposed viewpoint of a vending machine (2005–9), was followed by *Escenas de matrimonio* ("Scenes from a Marriage," 2007–10), a coarse comedy composed of vignettes featuring five ill-matched couples. Both titles consist of short sketches some five minutes long cut together to fit a fast-paced and uniquely short slot of just 30–45 minutes. The most popular long-form comedy also belongs to Tele 5: *Aída* (2005–), a working-class title spun off from the groundbreaking *7 Vidas* (1999–2006, the first Spanish sitcom to recreate US production processes), has survived even the loss of its titular star. Carmen Machi, who played a feisty cleaning lady, left the show and landed a starring role as a foul-mouthed right-wing politician in Almodóvar's short *La concejala antropófaga* ("The Cannibalistic Councilor"), which was itself (as mentioned in the previous chapter) a spin-off from the director's feature, *Los abrazos rotos*.

TVE-1, meanwhile, made a successful return to a long-lost genre, the prime-time soap. With its thirty-sixth and final episode airing on February 2, 2009, as the new season of shows began to air, *Herederos* ("Inheritors") starred veteran Concha Velasco as the matriarch of a wealthy troubled family cohabiting *Dallas*-style in the traditionalist setting of a bull ranch. TVE's prize-winning period shows in prime time and daytime (*Cuéntame cómo pasó* ["Tell Me How It Happened," 2001–], on hiatus in spring 2009, and rare homegrown *telenovela Amar en tiempos revueltos* ["Loving in Troubled Times," 2005–]) also show no signs of running out of steam. *Cuéntame* is one of the rare Spanish-originated formats that have been exported abroad, to both Europe and Latin America.

TV Texts

Returning to the premieres of the Spring 2009 season, it is clear that they not only boast the luxury casts of recent TV successes (with film stars prominent among them), but also offer audiences innovative themes and approaches that have successfully caught their interest and stress a cultural proximity to the viewer that imported shows necessarily lack. The first theme is a continuing exploration of Spanish national history, both distant and recent; the second is the fractured family, particularly caused by missing mothers; and the third is nostalgia for close community, whether its location is urban or rural. For the purpose of this survey I focus on the four titles in this exceptionally rich season, which, because of their initial success, seem most likely to survive into further seasons for their respective networks.

The most notable, indeed unprecedented, trend in Spanish TV for spring 2009 is the first depiction of King Juan Carlos I in fictional form. True to the spirit of counterprogramming (and risking repeating even itself), Antena 3 broadcast two fully cinematic miniseries on similar themes focusing on the figure of the monarch: *23-F: historia de una traición* ("February 23: The History of a Betrayal") explored national drama through a mystery format, in which the present-day children of historical actors in Tejero's failed coup d'état in 1981 explore their parents' murky past; *Una bala para el Rey* ("A Bullet for the King") used thriller technique (complete with jittery handheld camera and slippery zoom) to dramatize a failed assassination attempt on the King in Mallorca in 1995. Both were eclipsed by TVE-1's two part *23-F: El día más difícil del Rey* ("February 23: The King's Most Difficult Day"), which won the highest audience ever for a miniseries in Spain: 6.5 million on the first night and almost 7 million on the second (FórmulaTV.com 2009b). Just days later the miniseries was released on DVD, supported by period documentary and news footage from the public broadcaster's unique library, which had also been broadcast immediately after the series had aired.

Javier Pons, the director general of TVE, said at the press conference promoting the show that the public broadcaster had been inspired by the British feature *The Queen* (Ruiz del Árbol 2009). And *23-F* is, if anything, more sober and less like a caricature than its model. As the king, Lluís Homar (the male lead in *Los abrazos rotos*, examined in chapter 3 of this book and released just days after the miniseries screened) does not share the uncanny resemblance of Helen Mirren to the British sovereign, but his portrayal combines sympathy for a man betrayed by the generals

Armida and Millans del Bosch, whom he believes to be his friends, with respect for the man who remains Spain's head of state. And while the scenes showing the royal family, especially the father's relation with the young prince (the latter interrupts vital business, even as he is groomed for the throne), can be saccharine, the series also reveals the naivety and inexperience of the king and his lengthy hesitation before making his climactic TV appearance in support of democracy. The military maneuvers of the *golpistas* (conspirators) are convincingly depicted, and the use of a timeline device, counting down the hours, successfully draws on the conventions of the thriller or action movie.

Given that this is the first time the royal family has been impersonated in TV fiction, *23-F* does not seem overreverent. The fact that the attempted coup d'état surprises the king in his squash clothes (a typically accurate historical detail) lends some incongruity to early scenes; while the elaborate preparations for the royal breakfast that play under the credits (anonymous hands pressing oranges and preparing tasty treats) suggest that the attempted coup interrupted not just everyday domesticity but also a life of pampered (and perhaps blinkered) privilege.

The second historical fiction I discuss also comes from TVE-1 and is equally innovative in a very different format. *Águila Roja* ("Red Eagle") premiered on Thursday, February 19, at 10 PM after lengthy delays and reshoots that were reported by invaluable specialist website FórmulaTV.com (2009a). (Typically, the first episode takes place at Christmas, hardly appropriate for the date of the broadcast.) Set somewhat vaguely in a period described alternately as "the Golden Age" or "the 17th century," which presumably seeks to remind viewers of the hypersuccessful feature *Alatriste* (Díaz Yanes, 2006), the format combines swashbuckling costume drama with sword and sorcery fantasy and even martial arts action. Gonzalo de Montalvo (handsome David Janer) is a mild-mannered schoolmaster whose wife is unjustly imprisoned, tortured, and murdered by the wicked Comisario, himself in league with a mysterious hooded fraternity (reminiscent of the Priory of Sion in *The Da Vinci Code*) that is conspiring against the (unnamed) king. On the death of his wife, Gonzalo, who is now a single parent to his young son Alonso, transforms himself into the masked superhero of the title, whose good deeds are marked by a single scarlet feather he leaves on the scene. Vowing to avenge his wife, he also comes into contact with his sister-in-law and an unlikely childhood friend, now ennobled by marriage: the sexy Lucrecia, Marquesa de Santillana, who lodges her own pampered infant in Gonzalo's ruinous school.

While the periodization is deliberately hazy and the script makes no attempt to mimic Golden Age diction, *Águila Roja* remains a quality product with high production values, shot on permanent interior sets some three thousand square meters in extent and with close attention to costume and art design. Produced by a team at Globomedia (including veteran Daniel Écija), it also marks a clear departure from the contemporary titles that made that company's and executive's name in the 1990s, such as the pioneering workplace drama *Periodistas* ("Journalists," 1998–2002). Yet although it exploits to the hilt the traditional pleasures of period fiction, *Águila Roja* seeks to distance itself from the tropes of costume drama familiar from, say, the BBC. Thus the series' genre is clearly mixed and its tone uneven. There are from the start some quite graphic scenes of violence and nudity (a shower scene featuring Janer, posted by TVE itself, quickly became a favorite on YouTube [2009]) and the shooting style boasts handheld camera, quick edits, and even occasional jump cuts.

While the Robin Hood–style ethics of the series is transparent (in the first episode the masked hero distributes bread to the poor), as the season developed, more emphasis was placed on class conflict (the snooty aristocrat in the poor boys' school) and on the several child actors. With this unexpectedly successful title, then, distributor TVE has thus bet on the survival of the threatened "family audience," just as producer Globomedia has returned to its roots: the company's groundbreaking *Médico de familia* ("Family Doctor," shown on Tele 5, 1995–99) also took care to target all age groups. The generalist strategy clearly worked. With its second episode, the most popular new fiction increased its share to 26.5 percent, with the most-watched "golden moment" attracting almost 6 million viewers at a late 10:56 PM (FórmulaTV.com 2009f).

The missing-mother syndrome haunts another new fiction from TVE-1, the coarsely titled *Pelotas* ("Balls"). And if *Águila roja* is vague about its periodization, *Pelotas* is equally hazy as to its location. Shot close to Barcelona and made by El Terrat (the company founded by successful comedian and chat show host Andreu Buenafuente), the series also boasts well-known creators in Juan Cruz and José Corbacho, the latter a graduate of veteran Catalan theater group La Cubana. However, satirical or scatological humor that works well on stage or even film (the pair tout *Pelotas* as a continuation of their successful feature *Tapas* [2005]) can seem labored on the small screen. And *Pelotas* has more than its fair share of proctology jokes. But what is interesting about the series (and what necessitated the concealment of its Catalan roots) is its promotion of nostalgia for an archetypal urban community that could be anywhere in Spain. At the press launch held in L'Hospitalet de Llobregat, southwest of Barcelona (where most of the series is filmed), Corbacho argued that the show was appropriate for a time of crisis (claiming audiences would appreciate seeing characters even worse off than themselves), while director general Javier Pons praised the "everydayness" of the title and its role within TVE's new emphasis on quality fiction (FórmulaTV.com 2009c).

Pelotas's premise is as follows. Florencio (Angel de Andrés López, respected theater and film veteran, still best known to Hispanists as Carmen Maura's boorish husband in Almodóvar's *¿Qué he hecho yo para merecer esto?* ("What Have I Done to Deserve This?," 1984) plays the chairman of a low-ranking football club in a close-knit urban neighborhood. On the death of his wife, caused by a nose job that is botched by the hospital, his estranged daughter Nieves moves in with him. Meanwhile the trainer of the football team, Chechu, experiences family conflicts with wife Bea and their own teenage daughter.

As the title suggests, *Pelotas* revolves around rituals of male bonding, most especially the passions of Sunday-morning matches against rival teams. And there are frequent sequences in the all-male bar. Yet it is striking how *machista* jocularity is consistently undercut by feminine melancholy. The first, downbeat episode takes place under the shadow of the missing mother; and unrepentant patriarch Flo struggles, even while mourning his wife, to adjust to the new challenge of cohabiting with his estranged adult daughter (one nicely observed detail is his embarrassment at hanging out her skimpy underwear on the washing line under the noses of prying neighbors). Later episodes explore female fantasies (the late wife had longed to have sex with a black man) and menstruation (Chechu forbids his daughter to play football when she first gets her period).

Pelotas's exploration of race and immigration, like its apparently stereotypical approach to gender, is in fact double edged. While at first the Spanish footballers display crudely racist attitudes toward a recently arrived (but highly skilled) player whom they brand a "chino" (actually Korean), in subsequent episodes a touching romance develops between the culturally displaced but dignified East Asian (who is even given some dialogue in his native tongue) and Flo's attractively independent young daughter, now working as a tour guide in the unnamed city.

Scheduled for prime time on Monday (opposite Antena 3's attention grabbing miniseries), *Pelotas* gained the lowest ratings of the shows I discuss here. Although it premiered with an encouraging 17.6 percent share and 3.4 million viewers

(FórmulaTV.com 2009d), by the fifth episode it had fallen to a record low audience of 2.351 million. While the fact that it faced competition that night from the first episode of Antena 3's excellent miniseries on Francoist child star Marisol may not have helped, the lack of continuity in the evolution of *Pelotas*'s characters may also have played a part in the failure to sustain viewers' interest. For example, while Flo mourns his wife sincerely in the first episode (like Gonzalo in *Águila Roja*), by the second he is renewing an affair with an old girlfriend, who is inexplicably impatient for sex with the disturbingly overweight de Andrés.

Character construction is perhaps the strongest suit of my final title, the first not shown by the resurgent TVE, which is based, like *Pelotas*, on the return to a mythical community, in this case rural Asturias. Antena 3's *Doctor Mateo* (rapidly picked up for a second season [FórmulaTV.com 2009h]) is based on the British dramedy *Doc Martin*, a fact playfully referenced in the show itself by occasional shots of a signpost claiming that "San Martín del Sella" is twinned with the (equally fictional) "Portwenn," the supposed Cornish location of the original. Produced by successful independent Notro (simultaneously airing another series on rival private channel Cuatro), *Doctor Mateo* gained the highest ratings in five years for a fiction premiere on Antena 3: a 26.5 percent share and 4.463 million viewers on

Illustration 4.1: *Doctor Mateo* (Antena 3, 2009)

February 23. In a grateful Asturias, whose local government had sponsored the show, it won an astonishing 38 percent share, even though local references seem mostly restricted to the cast's frequent drinking of cider. And, like *Águila Roja*, *Doctor Mateo* proved especially popular with the younger viewers sought after by advertisers (FórmulaTV.com 2009d). With its second episode on March 2, it led once more in Sunday prime time, even against Tele 5's veteran warhorse *Aída* (FórmulaTV.com 2009g).

Antena 3's promotion for *Doctor Mateo* shows star Gonzalo de Castro standing stiffly in front of, first, a New York street scene and, second, the green valleys and snowy mountains of Asturias. The tagline is "De la Quinta Avenida al quinto pino" (perhaps best translated as, "From midtown Manhattan to the middle of nowhere") (Antena 3 2009). The familiar fish-out-of-water motif has de Castro's humorless medic retreat from a stressful life as a surgeon in the US metropolis to the village of his childhood, where his modest role as general practitioner is disrupted by a supporting cast of rural eccentrics (the baker, barkeeper, plumber, etc.). Sticking quite closely to the original British plotlines, the first episode focuses on an embarrassing medical condition shared by the local rich man and his overlubricated wife; the second on a deluded farmer, apparently visited by extraterrestrials; and the third on the finicky policeman's wooing of the new librarian. These gently comic threads are skillfully interwoven with the main romantic motif: the sexual tension between the repressed doctor and the sensual schoolteacher, Adriana, played by film star Natalia Verbeke.

The performances by both the dignified Gonzalo de Castro (best known as Blanca Portillo's partner in several seasons of the superior sitcom *7 Vidas*) and the charming Verbeke (*El otro lado de la cama* ["The Other Side of the Bed," Martínez Lázaro, 2002]) surpass the British originals in dramatic depth and range (Martin Clunes seemed merely glum by comparison). And in spite of a shoot apparently plagued by rain (FórmulaTV.com 2009e), the Asturias locations look luminous as shot by respected film veteran José Luis Alcaine. Even the credit sequence is typically smart and stylish: a surgeon sewing up a wound dissolves into a fisherman mending a net; a medical bag opens only to release a flood of weed and water; and, finally, the suited doctor pushes over sterile white walls to reveal gorgeous green countryside beyond.

While *Doctor Mateo*'s rural idyll is surely as fantastic as *Pelotas*'s grittier urban community (and may equally provide a somewhat facile consolation in a time of economic and social crisis), the show is expertly produced, plotted, and performed, making it the most reliably consistent and engaging of the titles reviewed here. It may perhaps be an accident, but, in this sample of four innovative audiovisual fictions (all of which are more than a match for current film production), the only show that sees fit to highlight its authentic Spanish locations is also the only one to be based on a transnational format.

TV Futures

Although Spanish television is thus clearly exploiting general themes that resonate with national audiences (historical, familial, and social contexts that are often unfamiliar to foreigners), it is also evident that these fictions, which are broadcast free to air across the Spanish state, attempt to avoid any localist particularity that might limit their acceptance across the country. The miniseries *23-F* is necessarily set in Madrid, but requires no knowledge of the geography of the capital (indeed, it remains unclear where the king's residence is in relation to the city center where the main action takes place); *Águila Roja* is set in a fantastic territory whose spatial coordinates are as hazy as its periodization (one later episode even boasted a martial arts mistress mysteriously imported from Japan); *Pelotas*'s nameless city is, as I mentioned above, carefully denuded of the identifying marks of its Catalan shooting location; and *Doctor Mateo*'s skilled actors (unlike their equivalents in the British original of the rural comedy) make no attempt to reproduce a local accent. Regional audiences are of course already catered to by the autonomic broadcasters that come together under the acronym FORTA, and some of which (notably Catalonia's TV3, which I treat in the next chapter) are themselves major producers of fiction.

While the 2009 season seems especially rich and proves the continuing existence of a general TV audience numbering in the millions in Spain, such innovative production is clearly threatened by economic and political changes. At a day conference on TV fiction held at the Universitat Autònoma in Barcelona, industry professionals warned that the present economic crisis made it likely that currently generous budgets would be cut for future projects and that this would limit the size of casts and the amount of location shooting. Moreover, the Spanish government also announced in April 2009 that Televisión Española, now so successful in its fiction production, would in the future no longer be allowed to carry advertising (Gómez 2009). This radical change in funding means that the quality television drama that is now taken for granted in Spain, and remains so different in character to that of fellow Spanish-speaking nations, may become as threatened and vulnerable as the feature film production that it has to a large extent already replaced.

Credits

23-F: El día más difícil del Rey
Format: miniseries in 2 episodes × 90 minutes
Date of first broadcast: February 10, 2009—10 PM
Channel: TVE-1
Audience: 6,491,000
Production companies: Alea, TVE, Televisió de Catalunya
Executive producers: Pablo Usón, Helena Moreno (for TVE)
Director: Silvia Quer
Writer: Helena Medina
Cast: Lluís Homar (King Juan Carlos I), Emilio Gutiérrez Caba (Sabino Fernández Campo), Juan Luis Galiardo (Alfonso Armada), José Sancho (Jaime Millans del Bosch)

Águila Roja
Format: series (8 episodes broadcast by April 20) × 90 minutes
Date of first broadcast: February 10, 2009—10 PM
Channel: TVE-1
Audience: 5,013,000
Production company: Globomedia
Producers: Begoña Álvarez Rojas, Daniel Écija et al.
Director: Marco A. Castillo
Chief writer and creator: Juan Carlos Cueto
Cast: David Janer (Gonzalo de Montalvo), Guillermo Campra (Alonso), Miriam Gallego (Lucrecia)

Pelotas
Format: series (8 episodes broadcast by April 20) × 90 minutes
Date of first broadcast: February 23, 2009—10 PM

Channel: TVE-1
Audience: 3,418,000
Production company: El Terrat
Producers: Albert Espel, Hugo Mendiri
Chief writers, creators, and directors: José Corbacho, Juan Cruz
Cast: Angel de Andrés López (Flo), Javier Albalá (Chechu), Celia Freijeiro (Nieves), Alberto Jo Lee (Kim Ki Yong)

Doctor Mateo
Format: series (complete first season of 9 episodes broadcast by April 20) × 90 minutes
Date of first broadcast: February 22, 2009—10 PM
Channel: Antena 3
Audience: 4,463,000
Production company: Notro
Producers: César Rodríguez Blanco, Mauricio Romero, Olga Salvador (also writer)
Directors: Enric Folch, Manuel Tera
Writers: Pablo Olivares, Guadalupe Rilova, Mauricio Romero
Cast: Gonzalo de Castro (Doctor Mateo), Natalia Verbeke (Adriana)

Note

This chapter originally appeared, in somewhat different form, as "Media Migration and Cultural Proximity: Television Fiction in Spain, Spring 2009," in *Studies in Hispanic Cinemas* 5(1–2) (July 2009): 73–84.

CHAPTER 5

LGBT TV Catalonia

Two Media, Three Texts

While LGBT characters are widely examined in film studies, whether Catalan, Spanish, or general, they are less commonly analyzed in TV series. (A rare pioneering article from Silvia Grassi appeared in 2016.) For example, Alberto Mira's invaluable and encyclopedic *Miradas insumisas: gays y lesbianas en el cine* (2008) is, as its title suggests, devoted solely to cinema, and no equivalent study exists for television in Spain. Yet the television medium, with its familiarity and closeness to local audiences, engages a connection with everyday life that cinema cannot rival. This chapter will sketch out some theoretical differences between the twin media of feature film and long-form television drama, focusing mainly on the latter, and will examine three parallel test cases (one film and two series) that reveal both significant differences and surprising similarities.

We may begin with the feature film in order to establish a context for LGBT representation in Catalonia. *Carícies* ("Caresses," 1998) is a well-known, widely distributed, and much-studied feature film adapted from Sergi Belbel's play and directed by Ventura Pons. Pons is not only the Catalan filmmaker most consistently identified with the theme of homoeroticism (see Fouz-Hernández 2015), he is also arguably the most institutionally established filmmaker in Catalonia, a status confirmed by the recent publication of a book of lavishly illustrated essays devoted to him (Domènech and Lema-Hincapié 2015).

Nominally set in Barcelona (Pons inserts occasional traveling shots of recognizable monuments such as the clock high above the Plaza de Catalunya), *Carícies* recreates a series of abstract conflicts between anonymous couples who are provided with no social context. Whether straight, lesbian, or gay in subject matter, these episodes all document a generalized alienation and impossibility of communication, which, it is implied, is characteristic of the modern metropolis.

Ventdelplà (2005–10) is a series made by Diagonal, the most prestigious TV producer in Catalunya, and was shown on dominant public free to air channel TV3. Named for the fictional village in which it takes place, the show was based, like *Carícies*, on the concept of a celebrated playwright, in this case Josep Maria Benet i Jornet. Within the critically neglected medium of television, *Ventdelplà* thus aspires to the cultural distinction of Pons's cinema. Indeed the TV show shares much of its distinguished cast (Laura Conejero, Mercè Pons, Julieta Serrano) with the film. Taking as its premise the return of a city woman to the small town of her birth, the series presents the new version of ruralism in which, beyond nostalgia, the urban is always already present (a phenomenon ably explored in a collection edited by Joan Ramon Resina and William R. Viestenz 2012). Moreover, engaging as it does with many urgent social issues, the serial places its queer characters within a recognizable social context, which Pons's more rarified cinema fails to do. The question arises, then, as to what extent the two texts' depictions of LGBT characters are derived from the general properties of their respective media and to what extent they originate in the specific context of the Catalan cultural field.

Further complicating this analysis is a third and more recent televisual text, also from TV3, *Cites* ("Dates," 2015). Based on a British format also called *Dates* (Channel 4, 2013), this drama series comes closer to the premise and dramatic structure of *Carícies* than that of the communal ensemble *Ventdelplà,* focusing as it does on scenes of amorous connection and conflict between couples, both same-sex and heterosexual, encounters that are placed in the urban context of Barcelona. As a short-run series whose director claims it is borrowed from the BBC, still the paradigm of public service broadcasting (*Dates* was in fact made for the private Channel 4), *Cites* aspires more confidently than *Ventdelplà* to the cultural cachet of Pons's cinema. Such cultural distinction remains more difficult to access for long-form serial drama even when lent the imprimatur of a celebrated playwright. As we shall see, however, true to its medium, *Cites*'s performance style is, like that of the rural *Ventdelplà* and unlike the urban *Carícies*, naturalistic, drawing the viewer closer to a fictional world that is located in specific and concrete sites of the Catalan capital.

From Art Movie to Long-Form Serial

Carícies was Ventura Pons's tenth feature; eight of the ten were produced by his own company, Els Films de la Rambla. Yet Pons began as a stage director and his films frequently turn or return to theatrical and literary sources. The episodic format of *Carícies* thus picked up on *El perquè de tot plegat* ("What's It All About," 1995), which was based on fifteen short stories by Quim Monzó, and its self-conscious performance style is reminiscent of *Actrius* ("Actresses," 1997), which was authored like *Ventdelplá* by Benet i Jornet.

Like these last two films, *Carícies* evidently derives from a literary source. The frequent scene changes, linked by kinetic inserts of traffic speeding through the metropolis, loosen up the dramatic space but still preserve the original's claustrophobic interiors: bathroom, bedroom, or kitchen. Conversely the exterior credit sequence, with its city lights set to a sultry saxophone score, might seem predictable as a cinematic image of the city.

But as the film develops, its narrative and camerawork challenge audience expectations. In the opening sequence, the young woman, a victim of domestic abuse, suddenly turns the tables on her partner and subjects him to yet more vicious violence. And while this confrontation is shot with quick cross-cuts, in the next episode the camera slowly circles the young woman and her mother, a couple who are less spectacularly, if no less profoundly, unhappy.

Similarly, the dense plotting constantly changes the roles of characters whose dialogue is abstract and motivations obscure. The old woman, who has forgotten her love for the young woman's mother, is forgotten in turn by the brother whose wife she had seduced. Or again, the elderly man, whose expertise at cooking seems to generate inexplicable hostility in his daughter, is shown in the next episode having sex with a male prostitute, a more likely motive for the girl's anger. While Max Ophuls's *La ronde* (1950) is the obvious structural precedent here, *Carícies*, in its pervasive alienation and polymorphous sexuality, also recalls Chantal Akerman's *Toute une nuit* ("A Whole Night," 1982), which likewise takes place over a single night in a city (this time Brussels) and whose multiple partners are both gay and straight.

The overt anonymity of characters and setting does not hide Pons's commitment to Catalan culture, manifest not only in the exclusive use of that language (even Spanish-speaking actors retrained to speak their dialogue in Catalan) but also in his continuing artistic collaboration with some of the biggest literary and theatrical names in the country. The unnamed city is, as mentioned earlier, clearly Barcelona, with repeated shots of the revolving clock above the emblematic Plaça de Catalunya ("Catalonia Square"). And Pons elicits polished performances from his actors, whether they are attractive newcomers (Naïm Thomas, Roger Coma) or veterans of cinema and television. Julieta Serrano, the frustrated lesbian Mother Superior in Almodovar's *Entre tinieblas*, finally kisses a female lover on screen; Rosa Maria Sardà is touching as the mother who cannot admit the truth about the gay son on whose cash she depends. And she redeems the unlikely payoff in the last episode, promising to treat the wounded young man she comforts "better than a mother."

With its intricate plotting, meticulous shooting, and polished performances, *Carícies* thus aims for the prestige of art or auteur cinema. Likewise, *Ventdelplà* presents itself, even within the despised daily serial genre, as quality television, implicitly appealing to the authority of a chief screenwriter, Benet i Jornet, who has as many credits in theater as he does in TV.

Yet the serial contrasts in medium, manner, and mode with its filmic predecessor. As a long-form daily serial with no fewer than 365 episodes broadcast over seven seasons and five years, its virtues are those of repetition and familiarity, as opposed to the uniqueness and originality sought by the auteurist feature. Likewise, the theatrical stylization of *Carícies*, in dialogue, camerawork, and performance style, is contrasted with *Ventdelplà*'s pervasive naturalism, whether sequences are shot in the studio or in the frequent authentic exteriors. And while the first text's mode is one of rigorous abstraction (the big City, capitalized, as symbol of alienated modernity) the second's is one of concrete particularity (the new ruralist setting that is a very precise mixture of modern and traditional elements). Surprisingly, however, the very first episode of the series (before its heroine flees to the country) begins with shots of speeding city cars that could almost have come from *Carícies*'s linking sequences and with a verbally violent confrontation between two women reminiscent of the film's tortured dialogues.

These broad differences are acted out in the representation of LGBT characters in the two texts. In *Carícies* homosexuality is nonreciprocal, violent, and perverse: the elderly lesbian cannot remember her partner, the mature gay man relates to the younger rent boy only through a mirror that reflects his own sex, and father and son enjoy an ambiguously inappropriate bath (to be fair, as Alberto Mira reminds us, heterosexual relations in the film are equally sordid and unattractive [2004, 533]). In *Ventdelplà* the central male relationship between

Esteve (Ivan Benet) and Xavi (Dafnis Balduz) is, on the other hand, not just reciprocal and mutual; it is also inflected by the specific social factors (coming out, continuing homophobia, the initial disapproval of family, and the final arrival of marriage rights) that *Carícies*'s model of generalized alienation does not or cannot choose to explore.

In a video montage of the developing relationship (across the episodes, seasons, and years), called by TV3 "Without Taboos" (TV3 2008), we can see in fast motion, as it were, the interaction of gay characters with both the fictional community in which they live and the long-form narrative structure in which they act and react. The final scene of the montage is of a climactic wedding. Here the authentic mise-en-scène embodies the distinctive nature of the series' setting and premise of new ruralism: ancient stone walls contrast with dazzlingly white modern furniture.

In this montage there are also interviews with the actors who speak repeatedly of their desire for "normalness" and "naturalness" in their depiction of their gay characters, whose marriage is said to be a first for Catalan TV drama. Josep Anton Fernàndez has warned us that "becoming normal" is a problematic goal for cultural politics and production in Catalonia where queers are concerned (1995). But the second term ("naturalness," used in the sense of "taken for granted") is significant here as a term that is both aesthetic and social, marking a convergence, whether desired or required, of performance style and social representation (what earlier I called manner and mode, respectively). The actors thus act naturally in all senses of that word.

Now it is a commonplace of television studies that the role of long-form fiction (even when it is not, as here, funded by a public-service broadcaster) is to work through social issues, guiding audiences toward pedagogic goals. And it is clear in this case that the audience (like the assembled cast) is expected to raise a glass of cava to the happy couple. Picking up on Alberto Mira's account of homogenization and community in the Spanish state in *De Sodoma a Chueca* (2004, 606–7), it would thus be easy (too easy) to dismiss *Ventdelplà* as "gay" in a timidly assimilationist or consumerist sense, as merely promoting a new normativity for a middle-class public. Yet there remains a curious absence in the show: Esteve and Xavi have come home for their wedding from the United States where they have long been living. In a troubling omission, then, the strain of continuous cohabitation (for the two men? for the couple and the assembled cast?) had thus not been worked through at length in the series (Esteve is not even introduced until season

4). As one specialist website suggests, *Ventdelplà* the series, like its fictional guesthouse, may not be as "gay friendly" as it might wish to think (Gaycat 2009). Certainly another Catalan long-form serial that was broadcast at the same time, *El cor de la ciutat* ("Heart of the City," 2000–2009), was more explicit and challenging to a mass audience in its depiction of gay sex.

Conversely, *Carícies*'s celebration of the nonreciprocal and the antisocial seems torn from the radical playbook of the "queer," which goes back at least to Leo Bersani's *Homos*, which championed same-sex outlaws Gide, Proust, and Genet who were (apparently like Belbel) so hostile to bourgeois domesticity (2009, 113–83). Yet the universalist abstraction of the film's alienation, which embraces all of its characters whatever their sexual preference, means it can say nothing in particular about same-sex desire or, indeed, about Catalonia. Like the backward-running clock that is so prominent in its final sequence, *Carícies* is suspended outside historical time and space and cannot distinguish between subjects that are socially, and not existentially, constituted.

Still, however, there is a poignant contrast between the main motifs of the film and TV show. *Carícies*'s final caress is temporary and provisional, a gesture of connection between two isolated characters who have only just met, and one that is staged for a select art-house audience. *Ventdelplà*'s wedding kiss, on the other hand, applauded by the series' assembled cast and anticipated by its faithful mass audience, is a sign, utopian perhaps, of a lasting transformation of everyday life depicted on and attempted by the critically despised medium of television.

From Long-Form Serial to Short-Run Series

A further test case for this positive transformation of the image of homosexuality (a process that might be viewed more negatively as "normalization") is TV3's later series *Cites* (2015), which is made up of just thirteen episodes of forty-five minutes each. Every weekly chapter focuses on two dates between couples who have met on the internet. The twenty-four characters are mixed and matched through the course of the series, in a similar way to those in *Carícies*. Thus, for example, Paula and Sofia (the first a lesbian neophyte, the second more secure in her sexual identity) hook up in episode 2. But Paula will go on to date a man in episode 4. She meets up with Sofia once more in episode 9, which I will examine more closely later.

Illustration 5.1: Laia Costa as Paula in TV3's *Cites* ("Dates," 2015)

On TV3's website for the series, its premise is said to be that of a cast of characters seeking sex, love, or a solution to solitude. After making contact online, they will now find themselves "face to face" with all their insecurities and hopes. The similarity to *Carícies* is clear once more, with the key difference that beyond Pons's universal and irremediable alienation there is now a possibility at least of a hard-won happy ending (the reference to "hope") (TV3 2015).

The series' sole director is TV veteran Pau Freixas, who is best known for hospital drama *Polseres vermelles* (2011–13), a rare Catalan format that was exported to the United States, as *Red Band Society* (ABC, 2014). Freixas also stresses that with this series' free adaptation of an original format he ascribes erroneously to the BBC (the Catalans took just three of the British dates as a "starting point"), he wanted to make a "warm" series. In *Cites*, he claims, appealing to the first-person plural of Catalan-speakers, that "we recognize ourselves" and experience the nerves, the romance, and the voyeuristic curiosity of watching strangers hook up.

Heightening this closeness to Catalan spectators, Freixas writes that Barcelona is an "organic" frame in which to place these stories. "We love our city," he says, and it lends a "perfect spirit" for "romantic comedy" (this phrase is enclosed by quotes in the original, as if signaling a certain disquiet with a genre whose status is unclear). He hopes, in conclusion, that "we" too, after watching this series, will want to go out on a date. This is because "there is always a first time."

Whatever the case, romantic viewers will not lack locations for their fantasized relationships. A further web page on TV3's site lists all the places the series was shot, from "the sea to the mountain" (a traditional formula for orientation in Barcelona) and from center to periphery. There is even a map showing where the series' characters meet, to which viewers are invited to add sites and photos attesting to their own romantic encounters. We are far, then, from the abstraction of *Carícies*'s anonymous modern metropolis or, indeed, *Ventdelplà*'s more socially grounded but fictional village.

Let us look more closely at a specimen episode, the ninth, which was first broadcast on June 29, 2015. The rather laconic official synopsis stresses the seriality of the narrative, relating it to previous episodes:

> *Fa molt temps que la Blanca no sap res del Víctor, però finalment avui han quedat i hauran de ser sincers l'un amb l'altre. També fa molt que la Paula no veu la Sofia, i també elles hauran de plantar cara a la veritat i encarar les seves realitats.*

> Blanca hasn't heard from Víctor for a long time but they have finally arranged to meet today, and they will have to be honest with each other. It's also been a long time since Paula saw Sofia, and they will also have to face up to the truth and confront their own real situations.

As the synopsis suggests, there is a rigorous symmetry between the heterosexual and lesbian couples. Both have met and had sex earlier, although somewhat more emphasis is given to the latter's relationship in this episode. Thus the pre-credit sequence begins with twentysomething psychology student Paula (Laia Costa) nervously waiting in a bar for care worker Sofia (Nausicaa Bonnín) as it rains outside on the city streets (both actresses have starred in art movies, but not for Ventura Pons). We then cut to another café where academic Víctor (a forty-year-old university professor played by Marc Cartes) is himself waiting for schoolteacher Blanca (Bea Segura). Conversation is strained in both settings, although clumsy, talky Paula, who spectacularly chokes on her beer, will prove much more effusive in expressing her love than guarded, lackluster Víctor.

The action then shifts to two new locations where each couple will experience a revelation. Paula tracks Sofia down to the launch of a lesbian comic at the real-life Calders bookstore in the trendy immigrant district of the Raval (the store was only recently opened at the time of shooting). Here Paula discovers that Sofia has a steady lover: the older female author whose work is being celebrated at the event. Meanwhile Víctor accompanies Blanca to the hospital where her dying friend has been taken for emergency care. After the visit Blanca reveals to him that she is pregnant from their earlier encounter. He fails to respond and she walks off alone.

The lesbian narrative is more positive. After the fraught launch, Paula and Sofia sit on a bench in the street, talk intimately (Sofia has been guarded so far), and hug and kiss before Sofia walks off once more, back to the partner whose existence she had previously hidden from her one-night stand. But a third lesbian girl then bumps into Paula as she sits on the bench. Rapidly changing focus and mood, Paula suggests the two of them get a drink. And in the last shot they disappear together down a typically narrow Raval street riding a single bicycle.

As in *Ventdelplà*, performance style is here relatively muted, attempting to establish a close connection with a TV audience who recognizes the settings (when I watched this episode in Barcelona on the night it was first broadcast I had by coincidence walked that Raval street myself just days earlier). Viewers are thus encouraged to identify with the characters, whether gay, bi, or straight, who live out their love affairs intimately entwined with a dense and varied urban space. Surely, the everyday style of the series suggests, we too could have a "first time" in the Catalan capital, even when, as in this episode, the sky is gray and the streets spattered with rain.

The parallel plotlines between hetero- and homosexual affairs might seem to coincide with the homogenizing tendency of *Carícies*, according to which there is no difference between gay and straight because each is equally alienated. But the naturalistic setting of the series questions this easy alibi. Thus there is a certain tension when enthusiastic Paula openly (too openly?) expresses her desire for the more guarded Sofia in the bar (gently touching her breasts) and in the street (passionately kissing her one last time).

The heterosexual lovers in this episode are more restrained and never breach the distance between them. But Víctor's presence in the hospital, say, requires no explanation, in the way that same-sex partners still need to justify their presence in such an institutional setting. By shooting on the street and in authentic locations as it does here, television cannot help but engage with viewers' real-life knowledge of the restrictions placed on queer people in expressing their affection, even in a famously liberal city.

At the end of the episode, and once more outpacing the glum straight man, the dynamic young lesbian (who has only just acknowledged the nature of her feelings) is shown to be immediately open to new encounters, new caresses. Unlike other obsessive lovers in the series, Paula thus wisely acknowledges that her first choice is unavailable. *Cites* thus generously permits its lesbian character to experience both romantic elation and, subsequently, clear-eyed realism. It is a possibility of everyday happiness seen also in *Ventdelplà*'s gay married couple but far indeed from the stylized anomie of *Carícies*. The latter allows only a single, final gesture of comfort, when the anonymous mother extends her hand to touch the wounded face of the equally anonymous young man.

To conclude, then, these three texts and two media have revealed both differences and similarities. While *Carícies*'s high-minded pessimism might be attributed either to its theatrical origins or to its adaptation into an unrepentant art movie, *Ventdelplà*'s and *Cites*'s qualified optimism surely relates to their common closeness to a relatively small Catalan-speaking audience who have access to only a restricted amount of television content native to their own language and culture. Yet the generic differences between the two TV shows, long-form serial and short-run series, respectively, are also significant. So are their distinct rural and urban settings, in spite of the fact that the village of Ventdelplà proves, surprisingly perhaps, to be as modern and tolerant as the city of Barcelona.

LGBT characters will no doubt continue to be represented in different ways in Catalan cinema and television. But the depiction and significance of future queer narratives will be played out against the background of these pioneering screen fictions that have already offered audiences, both select and general, the opportunity to learn so much.

CHAPTER 6

Televisual Properties
The Construction Bubble in Three TV Series

Brick Fever

The construction bubble of the 2000s, with its grotesque swelling and traumatic puncture, remains perhaps the biggest social and political problem facing Spain in the twenty-first century. And its causes and effects are complex to elucidate, with commentary stretching over multiple disciplines from economics and statistics to political science.

What I will suggest in this chapter is that one neglected medium to reflect on this phenomenon, still so deeply felt in Spain, is that of television. Strikingly, while no feature film has to my knowledge engaged directly with the question of real estate development in the millennium (although Álex de la Iglesia's *La comunidad* ["Common Wealth"] of 2000 was an early gesture in that direction), at least three TV series have done so.

As we shall see, these shows are as varied in genre (ranging from farcical comedy, via musical drama, to quality short-run narrative) as they are in cultural cachet (low, medium, and high, respectively). Moreover while the first two series were shot for and shown on a generalist free to air network, the third was intended for a specialist subscription service. It thus follows that, taken together, with their divergent genres, registers, and processes of production, distribution, and reception, the three series will reveal differing perspectives on a single phenomenon, perspectives that are directed toward varied demographic fragments of the Spanish population.

One characteristic of television as a medium is precisely this continuing (indeed unending) worrying away at social problems in real time and in collaboration with a mass audience. It is a process to which John Ellis in *Seeing Things: Television in the Age of Uncertainty* (2002, 78–81) gave the name "working through." The nature of TV, then, is to offer multiple versions or visions of topics that engage its diverse audience, even as it adapts itself in turn (unlike feature film once more) to that audience's shifting response.

Yet television might seem ill adapted to the analysis of social issues. As John Corner writes in *Critical Ideas in Television Studies*, the small screen is generally thought to focus on the affective questions "How does it look?" and "How does it feel?" rather than the analytical ones "Is it true? Is it false?" (1999, 113). Yet, as Corner himself acknowledges throughout his book, if TV is indeed biased toward vision and sensation, still the pleasures and knowledges offered by the medium are complex, especially in the genre of long-form fiction. Moreover I will suggest in this chapter that televisual emotion (engaged in different ways by each series) is by no means indistinguishable from cognition. As Martha Nussbaum has also suggested (2001), emotion, however dangerous and unruly it may be by nature, can in certain circumstances constitute a form of cognition, a way of finding out about the world around us. These series are thus, in Nussbaum's phrase once more, "upheavals of thought," entertainments that delight, surprise, and disturb their respective publics and thus provoke both the recognition of self and the discovery of others. This is an especially vital process of working through in the sensitive field of housing, which combines, uniquely, the domains of the viscerally affective and the technically fiscal.

Before examining the three series, let us look briefly at three specialist studies on the construction boom and bust that is often known in Spain in resonant and imagistic shorthand as "brick fever" ("la fiebre del ladrillo"). The first and most recent is Lluís Pellicer's *El vicio del ladrillo: la cultura de un modelo productivo* ("Brick Vice: The Culture of a Mode of Production,"2014). The very title here suggests a conflict between an imagistic and moralistic discourse (the supposed "vice" of excessive construction) and an analytical, economic register (the culture held to be produced by a mode of production). The economics editor for dominant center-left daily *El País*, Pellicer combines in turn a journalist's eye for the telling detail and emblematic individual and the macroeconomist's perspective on collective financial trends that remain less easy to visualize and personalize. Thus he begins with the appearance in court of the Valencian-born former boss of a speculative construction company, based in Catalonia and complicit with the Generalitat's president, who has returned from exile to face charges of fraud (2014, 23). His grandest failed project had been "BCN [for Barcelona] World," an unbuilt megascheme for six casinos and five thousand homes for foreign buyers in the province of Tarragona (2014, 24).

Pellicer flashes back to the company's modest origins before proceeding to trace its unlikely and criminal expansion by appealing to such resonant headings as "the remainders of the shipwreck" (of the recession of 2008) (2014, 25), "a land of property owners" (referring to the deluded Spaniards who had been taught to scorn the rented accommodation common in such countries as Germany) (2014, 27), and "the cutting of the cake" (by which agencies took ever larger profits while their clients accumulated increasingly unpayable debts) (2014, 32). A second chapter culminates in an unlikely but typically Valencian "paella party in the city of skyscrapers," when the same developer briefly attempted to extend his apparently booming real estate business into New York (2014, 74).

In subsequent chapters Pellicer follows the same discursive pattern: he begins with an emblematic person or moment and expands out and back to offer a historical and institutional backstory beyond the scope of the front pages. Thus an empty frame in a grand office on Barcelona's Diagonal boulevard points, through the eloquent absence of the portrait it once bore, to the identity of the now disgraced boss whose pharaonic dreams destroyed the biggest property development company in Spain (2014, 80). Or again, the plan for "homes with an airplane parked at the door" (2014, 111) signals the disproportionate global ambitions of formerly provincial Spanish construction companies. This was another megaproject, to be built in rural Mexico, which would include its own airline to ferry wealthy residents to and from their luxurious second homes (only one plane ever took off) (2014, 126).

Meanwhile, the moment in 2007 when the minister of housing interrupted an interview with a skeptical BBC journalist (2014, 136) signals the tipping point for a construction boom that would culminate in almost seven hundred thousand new homes unsold (2014, 153). The same politician would later embark on a whirlwind "European tour" to London, Paris, and Moscow in an attempt to offload the new construction and forestall the fiscal crisis that would plunge Spain into recession and EU-imposed austerity (2014, 169). Finally the "roulette economy" of Eurovegas (a US-sponsored casino scheme for which Madrid and Barcelona competed unsuccessfully) (2002) gives way to the more everyday tragedy of mass evictions for victims of subprime mortgage lending, as uniquely harsh Spanish law makes no provision for debt forgiveness even in such cases (2014, 229).

Pellicer calls the latter phenomenon (which gave rise to a radical protest movement) an "unending social drama" (2014, 229). And there is little doubt that this study, meticulously footnoted and referenced as it is, appeals to the fictional techniques of serial narrative in its use of flashbacks, multiple viewpoints, and human interest stories. In other words, emotion and cognition are knowingly braided together. Indeed the two forewords to his book illustrate these diverse approaches. The first invokes the Barcelona housing militants and uses such words as "scandal," "pillage," and "perversion" (Pellicer 2014, 7–11); the second, written by doctor of economics, speaks more mildly of the "economic cycle" of 1997–2013 with its "marked contrast" between an initial phase of expansion and a second stage of recession (Pellicer 2014, 13). The lexicon here is one of "concentration" and even "normalization," in spite of a final warning that Spain may suffer further booms and busts in the future (Pellicer 2014, 13–21).

A similar disjunction in style and content is found in a dual-authored book of 2013: José Manuel Naredo and Carlos Taibo's *De la burbuja inmobilaria al decrecimiento: causas, efectos y perspectivas de la crisis* ("From the Real Estate Bubble to De-growth: Causes, Effects, and Perfectives of the Crisis"). While the first author is an economist and statistician, the second is a political scientist. Naredo's analysis of the current housing situation in Spain identifies the globalization of a speculative economic model that leads to three effects: the polarization of territory (the dichotomy between overdeveloped favored sites and neglected wastelands), urban sprawl (the rejection of the dense and compact land use previously common in Spain), and uniformity of construction (the neglect of regional or historical styles in favor of blandly impersonal and commercial aesthetics) (2013, 13).

Going back in time like Pellicer, Naredo traces the current housing model to Francoism (when speculation and neglect of the rental and social sector set in) (2013, 19) and to the new democracy (when a continuing oligarchy, an absence of town planning, and, later, cheap and abundant finance from the European Union all fuelled both construction and corruption) (2013, 29–30). Naredo's economic historiography thus coincides with Leftist political critics who reject the Transition to democracy as a disguised continuity with the Francoist regime; and he is also aligned with current housing activists in his appeal to a biologist rhetoric of sickness (even cancer: growth proliferates like malignant cells) and in his negative diagnosis of a "brick fever," which has for the author a vital ecological dimension.

Naredo's coauthor Taibo also argues against the environmental deterioration wrought by the housing bubble but concentrates on Spain's loss of political and economic sovereignty to the European Union and the Euro, which he claims has produced a democratic deficit in many areas. Taibo argues, consequently, for a utopian policy of "ungrowth" ("decrecimiento"), whereby activity in areas such as the military, industry, and construction would be positively reduced, thus giving newly time-rich citizens the ability to rebuild social bonds (2013, 136). Here, he claims, the so-called "informal economy," already so common in Southern Europe, can give lessons in solidarity and sustainability beyond soulless capital accumulation (2013, 135). After all, writes Taibo, Mediterranean farmers have long planted olive and fig trees whose fruits they knew they would not live to enjoy (2013, 136). The analysis of fiscal reality (such as Spain's inability to devalue within a currency union) thus cedes to a lyrical evocation of post- or anticapitalism beyond the reaches of Brussels bureaucrats and Barcelona developers.

Naredo had earlier expanded his analysis in another coauthored book (the last of the three specialist studies of the boom I treat here), this time with Antonio Montiel Márquez, titled *El modelo inmobilario español y su culminación en el caso valenciano* ("The Spanish Real Estate Model and its Culmination in the Case of Valencia," 2011). Here Naredo illustrates his historical teleology (the alleged continuity between dictatorship and democracy) and his economic etiology (oligarchy, deficient town planning, and EU soft money as causes of brick fever) with case studies of specific urban developments. Thus the building of four spectacular office towers by star architects in outer Madrid, the tallest structures in the capital, is explained by the fraudulent double rezoning of the land owned by the megaproject's initiators: the powerful soccer club Real Madrid (2011, 41–42).

Montiel Márquez, meanwhile, offers a meticulously detailed account of the specific case of Valencia, an autonomous region notorious for corruption in areas well beyond construction and presented as the definitive case of the Spanish housing model. Here legislative changes and pliant or complicit local government combine with the rezoning of land (once more) to produce economically and ecologically devastating effects. One image reproduced in the book shows the unbroken "screen of cement" made by new high-rises that hide the sea in the small coastal town of Cullera (2011, 152). Conversely Montiel also documents the rise of housing activism by citizens unwilling to be "run over" ("atropellados") by new, unwanted development (2011, 127). The key term here is "urban [or town-planning] abuse" ("abusos urbanísticos").

What we have seen in these three volumes, then, is that the boom and bust of construction is such a large and diverse phenomenon that it resists definition even by academic or journalistic specialists in the field. Indeed, spanning as it does economics and politics, government legislation and citizen activism, "brick fever" proves difficult to diagnose. Moreover, in the studies I have analyzed here, scholarly dispassion invariably cedes to social commitment and rhetorical persuasion. Hence, if specialist nonfiction accounts of the housing bubble blend cognition with emotion, then we can hardly be surprised if television, a notoriously sensational medium, should do the same. Indeed we might consider fictional series on this theme as parallel to the nonfictional accounts that, in spite of themselves, seem destined to borrow the narrative tropes of TV drama.

Con el culo al aire ("Butt Naked"): Care in the Community

On July 4, 2011, Antena 3, a free to air national network that is a subsidiary of international publishing group Planeta, announced its new fiction slate (*Con el culo al aire* 2011a). Along with a prestige literary adaptation and a historical drama (*Toledo* was set in the Middle Ages), *Con el culo al aire* (literally "with your ass in the air," figuratively "left in the lurch"), a coarsely titled comedy, was also trailed. The head of the company's television division placed these titles within a corporate policy of diversity of genre (set against a supposed "monoculture" of standard TV content) and claimed that Antena 3 was the Spanish media company that was best surviving the economic crisis.

On October 27 the network presented the new series to the press (*Con el culo al aire* 2011b). Produced by Notro, a company with a track record in family shows, the comedy is said to be a "modern" series recounting the day-to-day life of people trying to survive and to do whatever they can to keep their heads above water. The comic tone is said to derive from "picaresca": a historically loaded term for the roguery or guile that Spaniards have employed for centuries to get ahead in a perennially depressed economy.

Further aspects of the show are its ensemble nature, its closeness to current affairs, and its moments of drama. These, it is claimed, will surprise and impact audiences, as the characters speak and act like people in the street with no taboos or censorship. This regular cast, profiled at the presentation and all victims of the housing crisis, contains no fewer than sixteen actors. Unlike earlier Spanish series

Illustration 6.1: Season 1 DVD cover for *Con el culo al aire* ("Butt Naked," Antena 3, 2012–14)

set in apartment buildings, such as the emblematically named *Aquí no hay quien viva* ("No One Can Live Here," 2003–6; Smith 2006a, 82–112), here the ensemble lives in a camping site (the major innovation of the series). It is a location that was once intended for temporary leisure and now serves as permanent, improvised housing for the economically distressed.

Con el culo al aire clearly struck a chord with the public, running as it did for three seasons of thirteen or fifteen episodes, each of which lasted an extended seventy minutes. The opening episode, broadcast on February 1, 2012, won an exceptional rating of over 4 million and a share of nearly 22 percent (*Con el culo al aire* 2012). Yet in spite of the vulgarity of the title, the production company and network stressed the series' serious ambitions. The executive producer claimed at the launch of the third season that the current situation in Spain "unfortunately" offered the show "masses of material," while the head of drama of the now rebaptized Atresmedia said that the show's perspective on the sad reality of Spain was one of "solidarity," a term frequently used by the housing activists (*Con el culo al aire* 2014).

Let us turn now to the first episode to see how the texture of the show itself conjugates these elements of comedy and drama, entertainment and social commentary, emotion and cognition. As Eva Velasco notes in her unpublished article on the series and its apartment building predecessors, *Con el culo al aire* begins with a pre-credit sequence set to a voiceover from dumpy middle-aged Tino (Paco Tous). As he walks and strips off his clothes he recites a text on the reduction of human life to numbers. He then climbs a staircase as children scream "Don't do it!," suggesting he is committing suicide. But the camera pulls back to show Tino simply diving into a pool.

As his voiceover continues, we are told that the cast are twenty minutes from the city with fresh air, green grass, and barbecues: "everything rich people have— but we haven't fucked anyone over [*jodido*] to get it." The show thus identifies itself politically with the radical *indignados*, who are later cited in the dialogue. The camera then pans backward and forward over the chaotic but colorful outdoor set with its modest bungalows and trailers. The still anonymous ensemble cast walk in and out of frame, the very image of a collective protagonist. The theme tune then kicks in, with its chorus of deprivation and defiance: "Aquí estoy/ Con el culo al aire/ sin pasta, sin curro/ y no le importa a nadie/ si vivo o respiro/ ¿qué más puedo necesitar? ("Here I am butt naked, with no cash or job. Nobody cares if I live or die. What more can I ask for?"). The camera then cranes up beyond this communal chaos to show in the distance the colossal new towers cited by Naredo as exemplary of Madrid's brick fever (the towers are also prominent on the series' DVD cover). In the middle ground an unsightly pile of tires undercuts the star architects' glamorous megaprojects.

The series' very setting thus confirms Naredo's diagnosis of Spain's real estate predicament: the polarization of territory between the shiny office district and the tacky campsite; urban sprawl, with that campsite linked to the city center by unreliable public transport (one couple are shown waiting disconsolately at a bus stop); and uniform construction, in this case modified by bricolage as the unwilling campers turn standardized holiday accommodation into improvised family residences (one child will be trapped in a Murphy bed). Ironically, then, the show's set-up serves as an illustration (albeit unwilling) of Taibo's "de-growth": none of the campsite's residents have steady jobs and all of them appeal to the picaresque guile of the informal economy to get by. And their modest lifestyles are surely more ecologically sustainable than those of Pellicer's fallen oligarchs of the construction industry. Even the pseudo-bucolic setting, removed from the city center, is reminiscent of Taibo's Mediterranean groves of selflessly planted olives and figs.

Yet, as the episode develops, much of the humor (and the drama) springs from the question of solidarity in straitened circumstances, a quality that, as we have seen, is promoted by both political scientists and television executives. Thus we are rapidly introduced to the varied households who are all equally at a loss. There is a pair of retirees who, having lost their home, are now reduced to living where once they vacationed; there are two young men, one of whom works as a real estate agent with no customers, the other is unemployed, and both have been abandoned by their female partners; the "marquis and marchioness," a snobby rich couple so down on their luck they can't afford to fill the Mercedes that sits proudly outside their shack; one family with an alcoholic mother; and another blended from two broken homes: a hairdresser mother and a *churrero* (fritter vendor) father with a Korean daughter. Finally the new arrival on site is Sandra, a recently divorced mother (played by María León, the biggest star and most accomplished actor of the cast) who offers her services as a doctor in exchange for free housing. We soon learn that she is an addict of self-prescribed pills, for which she has been fired from her hospital post.

Clearly these are not immediately pleasurable premises. They seem unlikely to distract Spanish audiences from the real-life dramas of, say, eviction-provoked suicide that they saw every night on the TV news in the period that the series ran.

Yet the show sugars the pill of economic depression. There is much broad physical comedy, as when the doctor literally dives into a dumpster looking for some money she has attempted to steal from the campsite owner. The show thus shows us (in answer to Ellis's questions) how the social issues it works through (in this case, homelessness and unemployment) look and feel.

However, the characters' picaresque knavery is not used against unseen oligarchs but rather to the detriment of their fellow subalterns: the "marchioness" blackmails the doctor when she discovers the latter's illicit pills and is blackmailed in turn after the doctor examines her skin condition, the result of a marital infidelity. Tino and family generously pitch in to help the doctor unpack on her arrival, only to demand a fee for doing so. One depressed divorcee claims that "the couple is just an invention to pay mortgages." Social relations are thus monetized, even, or perhaps especially, among those with no cash to spare.

Yet there are genuine moments of emotional engagement over the lengthy and fast-paced hour. We learn that one family was abandoned by its father, thus causing the mother's alcoholism, which is disconcertingly played for laughs; a teen girl, shamed by her stepfather's informal fritter-frying job, rejects his kindly offer of a modest birthday party; and, finally, the doctor's ex-partner arrives to take her beloved children from her. It is only now that collective solidarity shows its face. The ensemble cast, hitherto divided among and against itself, is shown testifying in court, each in turn, in favor of the mother. And in a ritual in the last scene (an improvised social bonding), the doctor, the new arrival, is thrown into the swimming pool. This is a visual rhyme for the opening sequence of the episode when it was everyman Tino who jumped in.

It is perhaps no accident that in Spanish the idiom "to jump into the pool" ("tirarse a la piscina") means to take a risk. But in the case of Con el culo al aire, the gamble is not only that of its picaresque characters struggling to keep a roof over their heads; it is also that of the series' producers and broadcasters who sought to make comedy out of national tragedy. The peril would perhaps be yet greater in Antena 3's next project, a series with a similar theme but in the unaccustomed and untried genre of the musical.

Vive cantando ("Live Singing"): Musical Barrios

On March 5, 2013, Antena 3 announced another new show, this time highlighting the signing of a single actor: María Castro, a sympathetic young star who had hitherto had an enviable track record for rival network Tele 5 (*Vive cantando* 2013a). Unlike the large ensemble of *Con el culo al aire*, then, this new series would focus rather on a single protagonist: Trini is described as a singer in a band who has spent the last few years touring provincial Spain before an unspecified "event" has brought her back to the urban barrio of her birth.

But the true star of the drama will be a space: the abandoned karaoke club that belongs to Juanjo (cinema veteran José Luis García Pérez), the boyfriend she abandoned long ago. This will be brought back into use as a meeting point for neighbors where they can unburden themselves and get happy. This provisional, improvised space is analogous to the camping site in *Con el culo al aire*, which also serves as a privileged, bricolaged location for the forging of new social bonds at a time of economic and affective depression.

The official presentation of the series, on June 6, 2013, gives thumbnail sketches of the characters (*Vive cantando* 2013b). Trini is burdened with a grumpy retired father, an unemployed former boyfriend with a taste for whisky (Juanjo), and a non-gender-conforming young nephew, who has named his pet parakeet Shakira. There is also (as in *Con el culo al aire*) a snobby, gossipy neighbor who will soon be humbled by the economic recession. Produced by Doble Filo (a company hitherto best known for the very different teen mystery *El internado* ["The Boarding School," Antena 3, 2007–10]), *Vive cantando* is, in keeping with its aspiration to middlebrow status, described by its creators as a "prime time dramatic comedy" (*Con el culo al aire* was simply a "comedy") and is helmed by a director known for his fiction films, Miguel Albaladejo (some members of the stock company of his features recur here in the new TV medium).

But if we look at the series' own website, a section on urban spaces precedes that inviting us to get to know the characters (Antena 3 2013). Thus, on a page called "Visit our neighborhood," we are invited to click and pan on 360-degree views of the local bar, the characters' modest homes, the rapidly refurbished karaoke club, and the small square of the series' imaginary barrio La Gloria, where the balcony of Trini's humble flat faces on to a communal space of social interaction.

In keeping with Ellis's general description of TV's bias toward "how things look and feel" and, in this case, echoing the catchphrase of one character, we are also invited to "visualize our lives." Viewers are advised by the cast on how to cope, say, with rejection in a bar by a prospective partner. And in a modest attempt at interactivity they are invited to vote for favorite songs to be featured on the show. As in the case of *Con el culo al aire*, the general public accepted Antena 3's invitation to spend the night in this new location: the first season led in its timeslot, attracting an audience of over 2.5 million and a respectable share of 15.3 percent. After two seasons and twenty-five episodes the series was not, however, picked up for a third outing, testimony perhaps to its unusual musical genre (*Vive cantando* 2014).

The first episode of *Vive cantando* is less explicit than *Con el culo al aire* in its reference to the continuing housing crisis. And its slower pace and more concentrated focus lend it a more dramatic, even melodramatic, tone. The opening shots remain comic, however. Set to a voiceover from Trini narrating her flight from the barrio in a failed attempt to become a star, we see successive fragments of a female body: close-ups of a platform shoe stubbing out a cigarette, of lips being glossed in a makeup mirror, and of breasts being tucked into a glitter mini-dress. Our vivacious red-headed heroine ("They call me Trini Turner") totters onstage amid a hail of feedback to announce: "Buenas noches, Alcantarilla." The bathos is evident. The real-life tiny town in provincial Murcia where she is performing is named "sewer."

Hooking up later in her trailer with a rare fan, Trini is soon disturbed by a mousy woman who proves to be her sister, a housecleaner stricken with cancer. Giving up on her dreams of showbiz success, Trini will return to her home neighborhood of La Gloria, which is clearly modeled on Madrid's Vallecas. This latter traditionalist working-class suburb is cited in the credits, and its perennially underdog soccer club is referenced in the dialogue. The family to which Trini goes back is (like the improvised households of *Con el culo al aire*) already broken. Her sister's husband has abandoned wife and kids for a job in France. And the neighborhood belies its name. As free-spirited Trini trips barefoot down the darkened streets, she is warned to watch out for broken glass and syringes.

The ironically named La Gloria is thus one of those neglected locations that have suffered from the "polarization" of urban space decried by political scientist Naredo, lying far indeed from the shiny towers of the star architects. But still, nostalgically perhaps, the barrio benefits (or suffers) from the density of land use traditional in Spain: the snobby neighbors immediately learn of Trini's return, complain about her noise, and wish they could move out to the suburbs (although by Christmas the economic crisis will mean they can no longer afford luxury foodstuffs whose visible consumption is compulsory over Spanish holidays). The shuttered karaoke bar is thus emblematic of a construction crisis that dare not speak its name. Indeed, having lost his home, Juanjo, the former owner, sleeps in the office there.

The series opens, then, in an apparent displacement of the economic boom and bust, under the shadow of death and despair. Hoping to help out her estranged family on her first morning, Trini manages to burn the breakfast, scorch the laundry, and accidentally kill the pet parakeet. Later it will be solemnly buried in a verdant park on a hill with a view of the distant central city. Juanjo, Trini's unemployed ex-boyfriend, wastes fruitless hours at the local job center. Trini's niece skips school to earn a few euros holding a board advertising a dealer who buys gold (she sees her grandfather slip in to sell some valued trinket). Trini's own repeated boast ("I have a record coming out in October") is shown to be a lie.

Yet beyond maudlin sentimentality, the series claims that emotion can be cognition, that feeling can indeed transcend finance. One plotline has special pathos. As his wife soon learns from a gossipy neighbor, the barman has sent a bunch of roses to Trini's dying sister, a daily customer. He passes this gesture off as friendly concern. What we finally learn eventually, however, is that he truly loves the sick woman but has chosen not to act on his feelings and thus threaten his marriage through infidelity. A sentimental education for both cast and audience, *Vive cantando* thus guides its viewer toward some ethical choices (the barman's altruism and self-sacrifice) even as it warns us against others (Trini's absent brother-in-law's egotism and irresponsibility). The story arc of the very first episode will thus teach us a lesson in caring: chaotic Trini, apparently unable to look after even herself, will finally take on the burden of her dead sister's children.

Here music is of the essence. Song represents not only the reforging of social bonds broken by financial hardship but also the transcendence of everyday trials in a neglected urban space. Thus, as Trini burns the toast (and inadvertently gases the parakeet), her young nephew and niece (the former sporting a tiara) dance and sing along to an apparently undistinguished techno number. It is called "Heatbreaker" by Auryn, a real-life band made up of TV song contest winners. Even the most artificial of pop phenomena can thus provide pure joy to the characters (and perhaps to the audience watching at home). Trini, on the other hand, had attempted "La Bamba" on stage to an indifferent audience in Alcantarilla (the song foreshadows the name of the shuttered karaoke bar back in the barrio).

But the most important song in the episode is "Corazón contento" ("Happy Heart"), a well-remembered hit for former child star Marisol back in 1969. The song recurs twice at the end of the episode. First Trini surprises her sick sister with a performance at the hastily reopened karaoke bar, helping her with the dance steps and singing together to the assembled cast (the scene is parallel to the final communal scene of the swimming pool in *Con el culo al aire*). But Trini later sings "Corazón contento" once more as her sister lies dying in bed, surrounded by her children. Here Trini's unaccompanied version fades into the original professional recording by Marisol, an individual performance in the present thus fusing with a much-loved collective memory of the past.

The mindlessly optimistic lyrics of the pop song (which speak of the sun flooding through a window) might seem facile consolation for economic depression, let alone for early mortality. But just as *Vive cantando* refurbishes traditional spaces to forge new social bonds in a depressed urban environment, so the series repurposes popular songs to offer emotional solace in a newly unforgiving culture, one undermined by abuses that are at once personal and national.

Crematorio ("Crematory"): Criminal Histories

Even more than *Vive cantando*, *Crematorio*, the first drama made for Spain's premium subscription channel Canal+, is focused on a single protagonist. Unlike those of the first two series discussed in this chapter, the poster and DVD cover for *Crematorio* show only one person, José Sancho's architect–cum–property developer Rubén Bertomeu. His looming, gloomy face is superimposed over the high-rise skyline of coastal towers at night.

At the press launch of the series, which is limited to just eight episodes of fifty minutes each in duration, Canal+ invokes Rafael Chirbes, the prize-winning author of the novel from which the project is adapted (the enigmatic title remains the same), and Fernando Bovaira, an executive producer whose company MOD is best known for ambitious feature films directed by Alejandro Amenábar and Alejandro González Iñárritu (*Crematorio* 2010a). This TV megaproject, the long-awaited first fiction series of a France-based premium cabler, thus appeals in traditional style to more prestigious media in order to lay claim to distinction: namely, literature and film. On the back of the DVD, the critic of *El País* is also cited as saying the show possesses "cinema quality."

Veteran star Sancho comes himself with a distinguished record in film and legitimate theater, while the series' two directors also boast credits in feature film. Making a further bid for the textual and psychological complexity typical of transnational quality TV (see Mittell 2015), Bovaira claims his show is not, as it would appear, simply "a critique of Spanish urbanism," while Sancho says his deeply unsympathetic character is "neither a saint nor a demon." (The DVD case puts it more plainly: "A series about corruption in Spain.")

Crematorio also achieves its aura of distinction by refusing to repeat the distinguishing features of Spanish TV series, which, as we have seen, tend to be ensemble shows that blend drama and comedy and whose episodes extend for over an hour. Meanwhile the focus on a single "difficult man" as protagonist identifies this novel project with the US pattern of quality cable, familiar to elite audiences in Spain and much praised by newspapers such as *El País* that are dismissive of local TV production. Rubén Bertomeu will thus be Canal+'s version of Tony Soprano or Don Draper.

Unlike HBO's mobster or AMC's advertising executive, however, the Spanish antihero is a property developer. And the producers later stressed that the profession and story were emblematic of recent Spanish history: this is the portrait of a Spain in which boundless greed and a mistaken conception of progress end up consuming everything; or, again, the show is said to be an "X-ray" of the country over the last fifteen years: a time of (illusory) economic miracle and get rich quick schemes (*Crematorio* 2010b). It was further claimed that *Crematorio*'s premise (the background to urban corruption "in our country") was unprecedented in a Spanish series.

Like the producers, the head of the distributor Canal+ also explicitly celebrated *Crematorio*'s "quality" and "difference," calling attention to the special care taken over scripting, casting, rehearsal, photography, art direction, and music, an interest that was fully consistent with the channel's "brand" (*Crematorio* 2011). Yet it might be suggested that Canal+ is reproducing in a TV environment the globalizing elements that Naredo critiqued in the construction business that is the series' subject. Thus the cabler promotes polarization between its own premium properties and despised everyday projects such as those of the free to air networks like Antena 3; and it pursues uniformity through the rejection of Spanish vernacular styles and the imitation of prize-winning US models.

If we turn to the visual texture of the show, this bid for quality and difference is clear. While *Con el culo al aire* and *Vive cantando* begin with a pre-credit hook (the dramatic swimming pool dive, the disastrous musical number), the opening episode of *Crematorio* (first shown on March 7, 2011) opens modestly in medias res with two men talking. The setting is an empty restaurant with a view over a colorless sea. One man will prove to be the grizzled protagonist (addressed formally here as "architect"), the other a Russian mafioso who will barely reappear in the fifty minutes that follow. With its downbeat dialogue and muted performance style, Canal+'s innovative project thus rejects from the start any too-evident pleasure, humor, and even drama (there will be a brief moment of spectacular violence later). In the series' washed-out color photography, the Mediterranean, even as shot here in the authentic locations of Alicante, Valencia, has rarely looked so gray.

Crematorio signals, then, that its elite audience's gratification will derive, initially at least, more from cognition than emotion. And it goes on to set out a narrative of construction boom and bust that coincides exactly with the economists and political scientists I cited at the start of this chapter. Thus, in the series' present, Rubén is the all-powerful property developer of the fictional "Mediterranean" town of Misent (the name is clearly Catalan or Valencian). His business traps in its tentacles police, politicians, and the criminal mafia we saw in the first scene. In the future he plans a pharaonic megaproject, comparable to those of any of Pellicer's oligarchs: the fictional "Costa Azul," with its several casinos and thousands of houses, will, we are told, place a screen of cement over the rare kilometers of beachside property that have survived thirty years of the developer's predations. Finally, the past is explored in repeated flashbacks to 1981, the beginning of a democratic era that the show believes (like the urbanists previously mentioned) is as corrupt and avaricious as the dictatorship that preceded it.

Thus we learn that the young Rubén has, since the eighties and against the wishes of his traditionalist mother and idealistic politician brother, concreted over the wealthy family's historic heritage of real estate. Orange orchards (emblematic of Valencia) have given way to holiday homes for northern Europeans. There is some overexplicit dialogue here: Rubén's sympathetic brother is made to exclaim: "You're talking about a lot of brick!"

Rubén's method here is already criminal, albeit at arm's length: in 1981 he got a henchman to set a fire on the family's then-fertile land, thus readying it for construction. His policy, then, has been literally one of scorched earth. As the brother says, once more with unnecessary emphasis: "You're burning more than the forest." *Crematorio*'s account of the nature and history of land use and urban development thus coincides with the ecological abuses stressed by academic specialists such as Taibo. And the Valencian setting (one distinctive rock formation would be recognizable to locals as belonging to the Alicante beach town of Calpe) coincides also with Montiel Márquez's view of that territory as the epitome of a policy of rapacious land development in the Spanish state.

Schooled in an anti-aesthetic aesthetic (a lack of the visual pleasure offered by mainstream dramedies), elite audiences were no doubt also trained to enjoy the unpleasurable pleasure of schooling in urbanistic abuses that they would no doubt decry. Yet, as the episode develops, ideological critique yields to melodramatic excess, revealing some close correspondences with the commercial series that followed *Crematorio* in exploring this topic.

Thus, just as *Vive cantando* begins with the death of Trini's sister, so *Crematorio* starts with that of Rubén's brother. And it is the familial (not social) conflicts between son and mother, brother and brother, that are the wellspring of the show's drama. This theme comes literally close to home: the brother's wake is held at the protagonist's ample residence with a retinue of sycophantic mourners in attendance. And one late shot has Rubén finally confronting his dead brother's body in its open casket.

Crematorio thus appeals to the emotive force of the broken family as openly as the two dramedies treated earlier. And if Antena 3's shows display nostalgia for now-threatened forms of dense urban sociality, Canal+'s drama is clearly nostalgic for a bucolic landscape (those orange groves) in which social bonds could be firmly, historically rooted—for their bourgeois landowners at least (we see no fruit pickers).

As befits its serious status, however, *Crematorio*'s darker tone leaves it much more obsessed with mortality than *Con el culo al aire* or *Vive cantando* (actor José Sancho would himself die in 2013 soon after the series was first seen). An early sequence of the first episode shows bodies spilling from garbage bags after a van has been stopped by the police. We learn that an undertaker, in league with Rubén, has been illicitly dumping corpses intended for the titular crematorium. This scandal threatens to unwind the skein of Rubén's complex, corrupt affairs.

A disturbing image repertoire of incineration (the burning of trees and bodies) thus echoes down the episode, raising brick fever to a deadly temperature. And this theme of homicidal corruption, barely hidden below the shiny surface of still-booming Spain, is crystalized in the strange and disturbing shot that ends this first episode. The dumping ground for the dead bodies proves to be an abandoned riding school that belonged to Rubén's family. And when the police investigate, they recover a mound of horse skeletons, which is seen rising perilously in front of Rubén's distant soaring towers, which form an ominous screen of cement by the sea.

Such disturbing images would not be tolerated in the more optimistic dramedies with which I began this chapter. The riding school reused as a human and equine cemetery is thus an eerie counterpart to *Con el culo al aire*'s jollier repurposed campsite and *Vive cantando*'s refurbished karaoke club. *Crematorio*'s bleak pessimism, so different to the hard-won optimism of Antena 3's shows, thus permits no possibility of social bonding, no renewal of an abused urban and rural landscape.

While that pessimism might be seen as politically positive, parallel as it is to the critiques of construction made by professional urbanists, it could also be read as pandering to an elite audience that could identify with *Crematorio*'s upper middle-class milieu and whose personal experience of recession was no doubt limited to the tragic stories they had read in the quality press. Certainly the series did not connect with a mass audience. When rerun in 2012 on free to air La Sexta a year after it premiered on premium Canal+, it rapidly lost viewers and ended with a rating of just seven hundred thousand and a share of 4.6 percent (*Crematorio* 2012).

However, even as it seeks to distance itself from ordinary television, *Crematorio* engages in spite of itself with the history of the medium in Spain. Protagonist José Sancho was not only a native Valencian (like many in the cast), chosen for his closeness to local lived experience. He was also warmly remembered for his more sympathetic role in *Curro Jiménez* (TVE, 1976–78). The latter was the definitive TV series of the Transition to democracy, based on the folk story of a Robin Hood–style redistributive bandit. It is a long journey from *Curro Jiménez*'s pristine rural Andalusia to *Crematorio*'s environmentally degraded Valencia. But perhaps, in the continuing career of an actor familiar to audiences over a period of decades, we can glimpse a parallel between two examples of Spain's belated and uneven modernization: the twin industries of construction and television.

Beyond Monoculture

It would be wrong to stress too strongly the polarization between so-called ordinary or mainstream TV and its quality or complex counterpart. As we saw,

Antena 3 was well aware of the economic value of originality. And with *Con el culo al aire*'s campsite setting and *Vive cantando*'s musical genre, it set itself against a televisual "monoculture" that is perhaps comparable to the architectural uniformity of the housing bubble decried by the political scientist Naredo. All three series also work through a new social problem that has no clear solution, either in their fictional world or in the real lives of the watching viewers, who have long since lost faith in a dreamland of property owners. Like financial journalist Pellicer, who also focuses on emblematic oligarchs, the series' creators visualize and personalize national tragedy through their chosen protagonists: a discharged doctor, a failed entertainer, and a criminal real estate developer.

Yet the three series offer different kinds of pleasure and knowledge to their respective audiences. *Con el culo al aire* proposes community, finally, as a balm for economic depression. *Vive cantando* suggests music as a temporary release from the grinding trials of the everyday. And *Crematorio*, less optimistic, at least allows us the schadenfreude of witnessing the downfall of the rich and corrupt (in the last episode a harassed Rubén will be shot dead by a smallholder he attempted to evict to build his megaproject). As veteran rocker Loquillo sings in the series' theme tune, he is "going down to hell ... burnt up by life." It is a long way from Marisol's sunny "Corazón contento." Yet *Crematorio*'s coastal towers are upheavals of thought and affect as well as of cement, asking us to think and feel the somewhat abstract and technical history of land use in Spain.

Crematorio's quick-cut credit sequence shows strippers, skyscrapers, horses, seascapes, and (briefly) a typically Valencian paella. But like the Spanish construction industry, this quality drama is much more globalized than Antena 3's dramedies. In the second episode we learn that, like Pellicer's real-life property developers, Canal+'s fictional plutocrat got an early start in Mexico (the unfortunate horses' stomachs were used to transport cocaine to Spain); and in the fourth a Russian soccer club owner has his land profitably rezoned (as in Naredo's account of Real Madrid's real estate development). The series boasts an unusual amount of dialogue in plausible Russian, subtitled in Spanish. Frequent bare-breasted scenes at a mafia-owned strip club–cum–brothel are reminiscent of those set in *The Sopranos*'s Bada Bing, an earlier morose and alcoholic hideout for difficult men.

The mainstream shows are more nationally focused and female oriented. On the DVD covers of *Con el culo al aire* and *Vive cantando*, six out of eleven and six out of nine of the ensemble cast members, respectively, are women. The gender focus as well as the localized perspective of ordinary TV, so different to quality shows' bias toward the middle-class men who pay cable subscriptions, are thus to be celebrated.

Yet in all three series, it is urban space that is the real star. And brick fever is concretized or crystalized less in the varied characters than it is in the provisional, repurposed locales of the campsite, karaoke bar, and cemetery, each ambivalent and problematic in its own way. The complex and contradictory connection of people to places, then, is the final lesson of these televisual narratives of Spain's real estate boom and bust.

PART III

(Re)Turn to Transmedia

CHAPTER 7

Toward Transmedia

Past and Present of Cinema and Television in Spain

Industry Histories

Anyone reading the Spanish press in 2009 could be excused for thinking that the audiovisual sector was in a critical condition. Journalists and filmmakers predicted the death of Spanish cinema, which had been identified by the director general of the Spanish government film institute (ICAA) as the "image" or "calling card" of Spain to the world (G.B. 2009). While the traditional foe of the film industry was always Hollywood, there was now also an enemy within: television. A Supreme Court judge had ruled that the substantial subsidies paid by the television channels to film producers, legally enforced by the government in its recently renewed Cinema Law, were unconstitutional. How, then, asked press and industry alike, could Spanish national cinema survive this new betrayal by the upstart electronic medium (García 2009)?

El País cited veteran Fernando Bovaira, producer of Alejandro Amenábar's successful feature *Ágora* (2009), on the negative prognosis for the film industry in Spain if it was indeed deprived of financial support from the television business. The article noted that TV companies had been obliged since 1999 to invest 5 percent of their income in film and that, in 2007, that sum had risen as high as 153 million euros (García 2009). The television companies replied that the practice had been "arbitrary": if filmmakers received subsidies from TV, why not sportsmen or dentists? Ironically, 2009 had proved to be a record-breaking year for Spanish cinema at the box office, with historical epic *Ágora* joining forces with genre films like prison drama *Celda 211* ("Cell 211," Daniel Monzón), teen movies *Mentiras y gordas* ("Sex, Party, and Lies," Alfonso Albacete and David Menkes) and *Fuga de cerebros* ("Brain Drain," Fernando González Molina), and Almodóvar's typically polished melodrama *Los abrazos rotos* (the subject of chapter 3 of this book).

Historians of Spanish film have commented that this rhetoric of "crisis" has been constant in a field known throughout its history for "unrelieved industrial decapitalization" (Hopewell 1986, 4). The repeated predictions of the death of Spanish cinema have thus been greatly exaggerated. Moreover, as scholars such as Josep Lluís Fecé and Cristina Pujol (2003) remarked of a now-forgotten cinema scare that had taken place as recently as 2001–2, a financial crisis for current industry practitioners should not be conflated with a crisis for all those groups who are stakeholders in Spanish cinema. To put it more plainly, unlike producers, spectators do not benefit from the making of feature films that fail to connect with the audiences for whom they are supposedly intended. Fecé and Pujol wrote rather of an "imaginary" crisis for a "cinema without an audience" (2003, 147–65)

While the polemic between the two media was especially acute in 2009, rivalry between them has been continuous since regular TV broadcasting began in Spain at the late date of 1956. And I shall suggest in this chapter, against received wisdom, that cinema has been for some time dependent on television, not just industrially but also artistically. In their monumental history of producers in Spanish cinema, Esteve Riambau and Caimiro Torreiro argue that the period since 1995, when the Law for the Protection and Promotion of Cinema first came into effect, should be called "the era of the audiovisual": cross-subsidies combined with the consolidation of "the great [media] conglomerates" meant that it no longer made sense to speak of a separate "film industry" and "TV business" in Spain (2008, 901). Using the evidence of parallel case studies of audiovisual products, I have argued myself elsewhere (Smith 2009e) that the convergence between the two media, both commercially and aesthetically, suggests that they can no longer be considered in isolation from one another.

Before tracing this somewhat fraught history, let us begin with a brief industrial survey of the current conditions of the two media. In all three areas of production, distribution, and exhibition, the decade of the 2000s had been a relative success story for the Spanish film industry. To take some statistics from the official source of the Ministry of Culture website (Ministerio de Cultura n.d.): feature film production fell to a low of 47 films in 1990, but by 2006 it had risen to 209; the audience for those Spanish films was 13.9 million in 1997, but by 2005 it was 21.29 million, giving the industry an enviable market share of 20.35 percent; due to the belated multiplexing of Spanish theaters, the number of screens more than doubled in the decade between 1996 and 2005. Although television had been instrumental in the collapse of cinema-going as mass activity in the late 1960s and the 1970s, it seemed that Spaniards had now been tempted back into the movie theaters in spite of the proliferation of supply on the small screen.

If this cinematic success has been somewhat obscured by pessimistic journalists or self-interested professionals, then the blossoming of television drama remained almost unknown outside limited academic circles in Spain, such as the research groups headed by Lorenzo Vilches in Barcelona and Manuel Palacio in Madrid. Since the early 1990s the production of quality local fiction, spearheaded by the *autonomías* of Catalonia and the Basque Country (who, as we saw in chapter 5, are more innovative in TV fiction than in feature film), has pushed once-dominant US series to the margins of the schedule. Milly Buonanno's Euro Fiction Group has noted that hours of local production nearly tripled between 1996 and 2001, far outstripping France and Italy, and that Spain has a higher seriality index than those nations, meaning that it produces more episodes of single titles for faithful fans (Eurofiction 2007). In spite of competition from the internet, those viewers watched more TV than ever in the first decade of the new millennium. In 1993 women viewed on average 223 minutes a day; by 2005 the figure had risen to 246, one of the highest in Europe (Rueda Laffond and Chicharro Merayo 2006, 449). With the exporting of innovative fiction formats, such as period drama *Cuéntame cómo pasó* ("Tell Me How It Happened," TVE, 2001–), Spain had produced a mature industry of prime-time weekly series whose production values were much higher than Latin American *telenovelas* and which could be compared only to the fiction factories of Hollywood.

It was Raymond Williams, father of British cultural studies, who first called attention to the paradox of the audience's early preference for television over film in spite of the former's "visual inefficiency" (1990, 28). Viewers were prepared to accept the technical impoverishment of the small screen, with its flickering black-and-white image, because the new medium was richer in its "social definition" (1990, 29). While cinema was confined to "discrete and specific works" shown in a "special kind of theatre," broadcasting was "general" in its content (music, news, entertainment, etc.) and was consumed in the "privatized home" in which citizens of the 1950s were increasingly invested (1990, 29). More recent theorists of television have stressed the medium's continuing flexibility. Milly Buonanno writes that "it is precisely because television allows us to switch between looking and listening, between involvement and detachment, and because it offers us both demanding and relaxing forms of cultural entertainment and social participation that it can claim to [be] an open medium" (2008, 41).

On a more formal level (but still stressing "openness"), Kristin Thompson argues for "redundant and dispersed exposition" (2003, 37) in television narratives, which, unlike classic movie plots, are often left without definitive closure. Thompson notes, however, the adaptation of films into TV series and vice versa (2003, 83–98). On an industrial level, the "convergence" of the two media has been dissected by Spanish media academics. Enrique Bustamante distinguishes between "vertical integration" within a single medium (when, say, producers take control of distribution); "horizontal integration" (when broadcasters increase their range of stations); and "multimedia integration" (when producers attempt to produce "synergy" or mutual reinforcement among their products or sectors) (2004, 88). In the historical survey that follows, we shall see how each of these questions (of social address, consumption, narrative form, and industrial synergy) has played out in the Spanish audiovisual sector.

After the coming of broadcast television in 1956, rigorously controlled by the state, Spanish commentators, more accustomed to film, proved nonetheless open to the artistic possibilities of the new medium. In his introduction to a book of TV scripts by pioneer Jaime de Armiñán—who would later direct the remarkable cross-dressing feature *Mi querida señorita* ("My Dearest Señorita," 1972)—one critic, who cites the already classic live TV drama made in the United States by creators such as Paddy Chayefsky, goes "in search of the televisual." He defines the medium as a "new and unexpected dramatic field" (Armiñán 1963, 27). According to media historian Mario García de Castro, Spanish TV drama (of which there was already twelve hours a week in 1966–67) was thought at the time to constitute a distinctive "third way" between theater and cinema (2002, 35, 25). As Tatjana Pavlovic has noted, it is ironic that the few surviving images of such early fiction (which was either live or wiped) are preserved on film, often in the newsreels that reported on the new medium for cinema audiences (2007, 9).

Curious hybrids also appeared in this early period, crossing the boundaries between media. Pavlovic, again, has studied *Historias de la television* ("Television Stories," 1963), a comic feature directed by Francoist film veteran José Luis Sáenz de la Heredia. This film combined the trends of consumerism and modernity with the changing role of women, as illustrated by its female protagonist, the enthusiastic would-be singing star and hopeless housewife played by Conchita Velasco (2007, 15). A lesser-known later example is *La casa de los Martínez* ("At Home with the Martínez," Agustín Navarro, 1971). A curious blend of sitcom and chat show, the TV version, which ran from 1967 to 1971, showed a "typical" Spanish family (albeit with two live-in maids) who entertained a celebrity in their home each week, granting them a key to their (televisual) house. The feature film of this show, which was made as the TV series came to the end of its run, begins with a curious prologue in which varied households are shown getting ready to watch the show: a butler announces to a posh couple that "the television is served"; a working-class man shouts out of the window of his flat to a woman hanging up the washing, alerting her to the start of her favorite program; and a family with eight children solemnly introduce themselves to the camera before settling down to watch.

This imagined community of television viewers is, in the feature film that follows, undercut by the anxieties provoked by the new medium. Old-fashioned Señor Martínez fears, given his wife's new stardom and the close attentions of the series' director, that he is no longer "master in his own house." A relaxing trip to the country, away from the bright lights of celebrity-plagued Madrid, is ruined when even the village hicks recognize Spain's "most heartwarming family" and insist on loudly celebrating the latter's presence among them. There is a constant refrain in the dialogue here that Spain has to "modernize" and "become European." It is a process identified with feminism, modernity, and television itself that seems at once desired and feared. Film audiences of the time (almost half a million saw this feature) were no doubt also disconcerted to see their domesticated friends, hitherto glimpsed in blurry black and white, displayed in full color on the big screen of their local picture palace. The "visual inefficiency" of television noted by Williams was here partially eclipsed by the technical superiority of a film medium that lacked, nonetheless, the "social definition" of its younger rival. Much later, television would return the favor to Francoist cinema: since 1995, TVE-1 has devoted Saturday afternoons to the screening of a feature film of the Dictatorship in a format known significantly as *Cine de barrio* ("Neighborhood Movie Theater").

According to Manuel Palacio, the 1960s and the first half of the 1970s marked the "Golden Age" of Spanish television drama (as the 1950s did for the United States). Commentators even lamented that, with the end of live performance in the studio, the "distinguishing characteristic" of TV drama had been lost (Palacio 2001, 86). Palacio gives a list of some thirty distinguished cineastes who worked for television at the time (2001, 87). And, taking advantage of the relative freedom of the minority second channel (TVE-2, which began broadcasting in 1966), future film directors such as Pilar Miró and Josefina Molina produced some of their "riskiest" works for the small screen, which proved to be a more open medium than cinema even under the Dictatorship (Palacio 2001, 132).

While Palacio states that TV fiction has always had a "distinct logic" to that of film and theater (2001, 143), he also recounts radical changes in the medium. For example, at the time of the transition to democracy, the studio-bound drama of the 1970s (one distinguished and long-lasting format was actually called *Estudio 1*) gave way to the "classic" prestige serials of the 1980s (often literary adaptations), which were shot on celluloid and used feature-film techniques (Palacio 2001, 153). Such series not only played a vital pedagogic role, educating Spaniards in the new ideals of democracy, they also offered some explicit space for radical politics, not always present in film of the period. According to director Josefina Molina, *Teresa de Jesús* (1984), starring Concha Velasco once more, reworked a Counter-Reformation heroine in order to celebrate "women's freedom of initiative" (Palacio 2006, 102). Faulkner has noted the complex multimedia dialogue between novels of the nineteenth century, their film adaptations in the 1970s, and the TV versions of the same works in the 1980s (2004, 81).

Yet TV auteurs thrived in very different technical and institutional conditions. Narciso Ibáñez Serrador's gothic series *Historias para no dormir* ("Stories to Keep You Awake," 1966–68) exploited the gloomy claustrophobia of studio sets to scare Francoist audiences; Antonio Mercero's more expansive and optimistic location-shot serials, some of the best-known titles in Spanish TV history, warmed the hearts of viewers in the dictatorship (*Crónicas de un pueblo* ["Chronicles of a Village," 1971–73]) and the new democracy (*Verano azul* ["Blue Summer," 1981]). While both directors also worked in feature film, they remain best and most fondly remembered for their innovative work in television (see Smith 2009a, 145–74). Much later, in a cinematic tribute to his low-budget TV dramas, five film directors (Álex de la Iglesia, Jaume Balagueró, Paco Plaza, Enrique Urbizu, Mateo Gil) were to join Narciso Ibáñez Serrador in making feature-length fictions that were released under the umbrella title *Películas para no dormir* ("Films to Keep You Awake," 2006).

As we have seen, feature-film production fell to a record low in Spain at the end of the 1980s, the same decade in which prestige TV series took on cinematic production values. But the much-delayed launch of commercial television in Spain at the start of the 1990s led to a perceived decline in quality and the controversy over so-called *telebasura* (junk TV). One unique figure in the crossover between film and television here is "popular auteur" Álex de la Iglesia. As Buse, Triana Toribio, and Willis have argued in their excellent monograph on the director (2007, 61), de la Iglesia pays affectionate homage to TV, citing horror auteur Ibáñez

Serrador in his black comedy *El día de la bestia* ("The Day of the Beast," 1995). And yet de la Iglesia's plot, in which a phony TV medium joins forces with an eccentric priest, is clearly a savage satire on private television, with the film's fictional "Tele 3" combining the names of the two principal real-life commercial channels Antena 3 and Tele 5 (Buse, Triana Toribio, and Willis 2007, 73).

As I have documented elsewhere, Almodóvar reveals a similar ambivalence to the small screen (Smith 2006a, 143–56). While his early features of the 1980s gleefully celebrate TV genres such as commercials and, indeed, popular culture in general, Almodóvar has continued to attack the medium since his critique in *Kika* (1993) of the new genre of reality shows, the supposed epitome of *telebasura*. The social presence of the medium is such, however, that it has remained ubiquitous in his cinema. It is perhaps no accident that both de la Iglesia and Almodóvar have dabbled (with mixed results) in the production of TV series that were screened on TVE-2, the minority public channel: El Deseo made working-class dramedy *Mujeres* ("Women," 2006), while de la Iglesia wrote and directed a sci-fi sitcom with the untranslatable title *Plutón B. R. B. Nero* (2008–9).

Millennial Media

In 2000 Richard Maxwell, the Cassandra of Spanish television studies, claimed that a multichannel environment would lead to "unprecedented demand for imported films and TV shows from Hollywood" (2000, 176) and a "decline in the quality and timeliness of domestic productions broadcast free of charge" (2000, 177). Fortunately, this has not proved to be the case. Writing in 2007, Vilches noted that, even after the introduction of two new national channels into a crowded marketplace (Cuatro and la Sexta), local TV series still dominated in the schedule over feature films, especially in prime time and on stations with a national reach (2007, 165). Moreover, Tele 5, then the frontrunner among all the channels, owed its success mainly to its home-produced quality dramas, a tradition that now stretched back to the start of the previous decade. It is perhaps no surprise, then, that the influence of television should be felt so strongly in the content of feature films of the new millennium.

Let us look more closely at the year 2009, which, as we saw in chapter 4, boasted a number of innovative new titles in TV fiction (Smith 2009b). As mentioned earlier, the most popular domestic feature films for that year, far outgrossing even an established auteur such as Almodóvar, include *Mentiras y gordas* ("Sex, Party, and Lies," a teen melodrama, boasting copious quantities of drugs and sex) and *Fuga de cerebros* ("Brain Drain," a teen comedy, reveling in crude jokes on such topics as blindness and necrophilia). While these commercial hits are often dismissed as mere facsimiles of their generic US equivalents (in this case, youth movies), unlike art films they receive little or no distribution abroad and are thus targeted at a uniquely Spanish audience. They thus encourage the national "social participation" that is for Buonanno characteristic of TV fiction.

Moreover, the principal selling point of such popular cinema is also domestic: the presence of young actors familiar to audiences only from television. While the Spanish edition of *Cahiers du Cinéma* complained of the "servility to television" that it discerned in the more high-minded of the current crop of Spanish film releases (De Pedro and Monterrubio 2009), the more populist *Fotogramas* celebrated multimedia integration with a feature promoting no fewer than thirteen of what they baptized "teletalentos made in Spain" [*sic*] (*Fotogramas* 2009). The mise-en-scène of this glossy photo spread is an unlikely classroom where young actors with "one foot in the cinema" (*Fotogramas* 2009, 104) are being lectured on the technical terms of television: a blackboard boasts such Anglicisms as "share," "primetime," and "late night" written in chalk. The brief biographies that follow in the text accompanying the image give the fledgling stars' credits in TV first, then in film. Rarely has media convergence been more self-evident.

A special case in this context is Mario Casas, the leading actor in both of the teen feature films mentioned above, whose previously supporting role in Antena 3's quirky ensemble police series *Los hombres de Paco* ("Paco's Men," 2005–10) was punched up to coincide with his new status as cinematic leading man (we will return to Casas in chapter 9). Hoping for synergy in spring 2009, the channel aired frequent cross-promotions of *Fuga de cerebros* in the advertising breaks for this series. Given that most Spanish films fail to appeal to the teenage demographic that comprises the most assiduous group of visitors to cinemas, the success of local youth movies of this kind, which attract audiences in their millions, is no small achievement. Such successes also contradict the "crisis" narrative of Spanish film promoted by more mature producers and journalists, who are, of course, temperamentally hostile to youth movies.

These films no doubt benefited from the disrobing of their young stars' bodies, which are kept somewhat better covered on television. And it is striking that, in these parallel narratives that cast the same actors across two media, it was the TV fiction that was more mature in its coverage of social issues. Thus the premise of the film *Mentiras y gordas* (which could have been unchanged since the 1960s) was that Mario Casas's character was a closeted gay youth, doomed to tragic death because of his unavowed love for his straight best friend. Yet in TV high-school drama *Física o química* ("Physics or Chemistry," 2008–11), one of the main training grounds for the casts of these youth pictures, a central gay character was treated with much greater sophistication, well integrated with his peer community, and even rewarded in spring 2009 with a steady boyfriend (most of the heterosexual characters in the series had failed relationships).

To take another pressing social issue, Spanish cinema has produced in the 1990s and 2000s a limited number of feature films on the theme of immigration. These are much studied by Hispanists abroad (e.g., Santaolalla 2005), but were often little seen in Spain itself. In the same period, long-running TV series such as *El comisario* ("The Police Chief," Tele 5, 1999–2009) and *Hospital Central* ("Central Hospital," Tele 5, 2000–12) produced a corpus of several hundred episodes dealing with the same theme, all of which were seen by audiences in their millions. More sensitive than feature films to changing social circumstances, these series also trace a shift in the representation of immigrant and ethnic minority characters from criminals and victims to authentic individuals. Increasingly "fused" with the host society, they now inspire not repulsion but sympathy and empathy (Lacalle 2008, 124–25).

Such series exemplify the concepts of Buonanno (2008, passim), doyenne of European TV studies. They embody cultural proximity, engaging a unique closeness to local audiences, and operate a process of "indigenization," whereby US genres, such as the medical drama or police procedural, are radically adapted and adopted by the various national networks. Serving as both cultural entertainment and social participation, they also employ Thompson's technique of "dispersed exposition" (2003) through the mouthpieces of their large ensemble casts and set in motion multiple plot strands that, unlike goal-directed movie plots, resist simple resolution.

Spanish television drama is also known for its attention to the past. Public channel TVE-1's weekly series *Cuéntame cómo pasó* (2001–) and daily serial *Amar en tiempos revueltos* ("Loving in Troubled Times," 2005–) have both investigated for mass audiences the texture (and sometimes the terror) of everyday life under Francoism. Such shows are at once demanding in their depiction of real trauma and relaxing in the familiarity of the fictional world they recreate for viewers.

Critics who complain of historical "amnesia" in contemporary Spain would do well, then, to pay more attention to this very visible national narrative, which is embedded not in cinema or literature but in television.

One unintended effect of the financial transfers from television to cinema was, as we saw in chapter 4, the rise of a TV genre that owes much in its form to film—the historical miniseries. Spring 2009 boasted no fewer than three projects depicting for the first time on screen the figure of King Juan Carlos. The most notable of these, and the most widely watched program of all time on Spanish television, was TVE-1's *23-F: El día más difícil del Rey* "February 23: The King's Most Difficult Day," which (as mentioned in chapter 4) recreated the attempted coup d'état which took place back in 1981. As the king, the distinguished theater veteran Lluís Homar combines sympathy for a man betrayed by the generals whom he believes to be his friends with respect for the man who remains Spain's head of state.

By coincidence, Lluís Homar also played the male lead in the highest-profile international release in Spanish cinema that year, Almodóvar's *Los abrazos rotos*, which premiered just days after the miniseries screened. Both texts seek to explore the past in their different ways and media. Indeed both contain scenes in which the dignified Homar engages in a kind of personal pedagogy with a younger male, who is (or will prove to be) his son. It is an educational process, which, as Manuel Palacio has suggested (2001 passim), is more often undertaken on TV than in cinema in Spain. It is perhaps no accident that 2009 also saw the publication of

Illustration 7.1: *23-F: El día más difícil del Rey* ("February 23: The King's Most Difficult Day," TVE, 2009)

two excellent books on the representation of history in Spanish television fiction (López, Cueto Asín, and George 2009; Rueda Laffond and Coronado Ruiz 2009). Another volume, published in the same year, which treats "discourses of the national on global television," also devoted substantial space to content from Spain, including the televisually rich *autonomías* of Catalonia and the Basque Country (Castelló, Dhoest, and O'Donnell 2009).

The link between film and television is thus industrial (the TV companies fund both media), generic (popular movies and TV series are mutually reinforcing), and artistic (young TV-trained actors venture for the first time onto the big screen, even as established film stars cross over to television, attracted by the steady work in series). The well-known virtues of television (its familiarity, domesticity, and cultural closeness to a local audience) might thus well be imitated in a film medium that has sometimes turned its back on national spectators and could learn valuable lessons from the small screen.

While critics and viewers have reason to fear vertical and horizontal integration in the audiovisual sector (which tends to increase monopolies in and across production and distribution), multimedia corporations have still produced some of the most distinguished work of recent years in Spain. To take just one example, Tele 5 has, through its production arm Estudios Picasso, created some of the best-quality TV drama and some of the most challenging feature films (such as Guillermo del Toro's *El laberinto del fauno* ["Pan's Labyrinth," 2006]). There seems little doubt that, in spite of persistent rumors of its demise, cinema will continue to be the calling card of Spain to the world. It is likely, however, that TV fiction will remain the mirror that reflects back to local viewers the image that they most recognize of themselves.

CHAPTER 8

A New Paradigm for the Spanish Audiovisual Sector?
Popular Cinema/Quality Television

Industry, Academy, Theory

I begin with two anecdotes. In 2013, auteurist film journal *Caimán* (previously *Cahiers du Cinéma España*) published a special supplement on the "Other Cinema." Transparent in their attempt to confer prestige and create cultural distinction, the various critics praised a young cohort of austere, low-budget filmmakers taken to be distinct from an assumed Spanish commercial mainstream.

In 2014 Belén Esteban, arguably the most controversial figure to emerge from Spanish reality TV, was sent by national network Tele 5 to Morocco in order to investigate social conditions in Spain's southerly neighbor (Tele 5 2014). Right-thinking commentators were horrified by this latest evidence of *telebasura* (trash TV).

It would seem, then, that cultural gatekeepers still have no difficulty in enforcing the long-lasting dichotomy between elite art cinema and mass trash TV. Yet other sources suggest otherwise. The annual survey of OBITEL, the Ibero-American survey of television fiction, was in 2013 on the topic of social memory, a theme particularly appropriate for Spain. And the Spanish section of the report, coordinated by Charo Lacalle, was entitled "Fiction Resists the Crisis." Lacalle records positive factors in the Spanish TV sector: average daily viewing in 2012 reached a new record of 246 minutes (OBITEL 2013, 280), with series fiction as the most popular format, occupying 21.8 percent of the schedule.

Showing proof of audience fidelity to local drama, swashbuckling romance *Águila roja* ("Red Eagle," whose launch was mentioned in chapter 4 of this book) was the most seen for the fourth year (2013, 282), in spite of government cuts to RTVE's budget that limited the length of its season (2013, 285). No fewer than thirty-two different local titles were broadcast, with a total of 36 percent being set "in the past" or "historic" (2013, 296); and the top ten exhibited a wide range of genres (from adventure and drama via miniseries and dramedy to comedy and fantasy) (2013, 299).

Social questions treated by these shows, said to be "highly topical," include prejudice against women and gays, the insecure job market, the housing crisis, and euthanasia (2013, 300). Of the only two titles that failed to connect with the national audience, significantly one was a failed version of a US original, classic sitcom *Cheers* (2013, 384), suggesting that foreign formats hold little attraction for viewers in Spain. Spanish TV drama thus both explored the country's past, connecting with social memory, and reflected on the present, engaging with urgent contemporary issues. This is a valuable combination that is not to be found in all territories.

If the Spanish television drama so eagerly consumed by mass audiences should not be tarred by the brush of *telebasura* reality programming, Spanish cinema, conversely but consistently, cannot solely be identified with the art movies promoted so determinedly by *Caimán*. In spite of media concentration on the precarious Other Cinema (whose audiences are as low as its budgets), the seventh annual edition of Madrid de Cine: Spanish Film Screenings which I attended in the capital on June 18–20, 2012, at the height of the economic crisis, told a more complex story (I give a longer account of another edition of this movie market in chapter 2). Intended, as noted earlier in this book, as the major professional event for the promotion of Spanish film to foreign buyers and specialist journalists, Madrid de Cine is organized by FAPAE (the producers' association), ICAA (the film academy), and other bodies, including the Madrid tourist authority. There was once more a *padrino* ("godfather") for the event. This year it was Enrique Urbizu, director of *No habrá paz para los malvados* ("No Rest for the Wicked," 2011), then the most recent feature to gain the best film award at the Goyas (or Spanish Oscars) and which I discuss later in this chapter. Representing Spanish national cinema, Urbizu gave delegates an evocative and informative talk on "the light of Madrid" high above the city in the tower of the Cibeles Palace.

In spite of a deep fall in production, things at Madrid de Cine seemed surprisingly positive. A FAPAE report at the event suggested that, out of a total of 199 features made in 2011 (the fourth highest figure in Europe), the number of titles screened abroad had increased (by 21 percent), as had the number of countries in which they were seen (by 15 percent). In Mexico alone distribution had risen to thirty-six titles, higher than ever before. Ironically, then, just as Spain boasts a greater number of tourists than it does inhabitants, so its cinema earns twice the income abroad that it does at home (in 2011 the figures were 185 million euros versus just 90 million).

Although Spanish cinema may be fully globalized, what I argue here, however, is that Urbizu's audience-friendly feature marked the beginning of an unanticipated trend: the reconnection of Spanish cinema with its own public. It did so via the neglected but popular genres of romantic comedy and (my subject in this chapter) thriller. As we shall see, the so-called *género negro* (police or detective drama) is a unique example of commercial film that is held by influential taste communities to be compatible with cultural distinction.

Independent of these industrial or quantitative trends, recent academic research, qualitative by nature, has also suggested that the dominant paradigm of auteur cinema/popular TV might be under pressure. As we saw in the first chapter of this book, Sally Faulkner's *A History of Spanish Film* (2013) goes beyond the auteur canon, rereading its titular subject by focusing on a new corpus of titles that are placed between high and low culture. Similarly Vicente J. Benet's *El cine español: una historia cultural* (2012) locates distinguished auteurs like Erice and Saura in their social context and juxtaposes them with supposedly trashy sexploitation and youth movies. Samuel Amago's *Spanish Cinema in the Global Context* (2013) likewise combines analysis of the artistic taste for reflexivity with the less cerebral trends current in the popular genres and the movie marketplace.

In recent television studies, meanwhile, Manuel Palacio has offered a minute study of the TV of the transition, arguing convincingly for the medium's decisive role at that decisive time as a kind of pedagogy of democracy in a new Spain (2012). This is a vital function that Palacio, the doyen of Spanish television studies, had previously highlighted in his general history of Spanish television (2001).

Beyond the academic sphere, there are signs that Spain is finally acknowledging the shift in the cultural status of television relative to cinema, which allows for the adoption of an aesthetic attitude toward the long-despised medium. After decades of virulently attacking TV, *El País* has boasted since 2012 in Natalia Marcos a specialist reviewer of television fiction (previous columnists limited themselves to humorous political commentary), albeit one whose perspective is restricted mainly to US dramas. Local television fiction was vigorously defended from the Left when it was dismissed by a Partido Popular politician as being simply a way to "pass the time." Spanish series now have an established festival (in

Vitoria) and (as mentioned in chapter 4 of this book) regularly host movie-style premieres in one-time picture palaces on Madrid's Gran Vía. Meanwhile the TV screenwriters association vigorously campaigns for recognition of their members' creative work. Tentative mechanisms of legitimation have thus emerged for the medium of television fiction.

If we pull back from such anecdotal signs of change in the Spanish audiovisual habitus, we might turn or return to current developments in the long-running scholarly debate on quality TV. From Europe Milly Buonanno has recently contested the overwhelming academic focus on the HBO canon, characterized as it is by novelty, edginess, narrative complexity, and cinematic ambition (2013, 9). This bias, she suggests, has served to conceal European traditions of quality that are based rather on cultural prestige and respectability (2013, 19). The new trend in favor of aesthetics in Anglo-American TV studies (Jacobs and Peacock 2013), meanwhile, has scholars arguing against the use of "cinematic" as a term of praise for quality television and championing a sensitivity to the distinctive qualities of the electronic medium, even as that medium is newly placed in the privileged aesthetic situation that was once reserved for high culture.

Adopting a yet more theoretical perspective toward the Spanish context of crisis (financial, political, cultural), we might also appeal here to Bourdieu. The latter speaks in the context of post–May 1968 France of the "dispossession" and "maladjusted expectations" of the former cultural elite. These terms are defined by Bourdieu's exegete Ivan Ermakoff as, respectively, "a situation where people do not get what they feel they are entitled to" and one where people "cannot fulfill their aspirations" (2013, 98). Like Bourdieu's *soixante-huitards* before them, then, the established film community in Spain employs a perverse negative strategy characterized by the "adherence to a behavioral script at odds with the strategic imperatives imposed by shifting constraints." In Ermakoff's words, the once privileged but newly dispossessed "draw on their stock of culturally shaped expectations and on their experience of past practices ... highlight[ing] the relative salience of symbols and past events in the collective memory of the group" (2013, 101).

The annual Goya ceremonies, which combine self-defeating protests of entitlement with appeals to once-uncontested symbols of an august past (ritual attacks on government policy and acts of mourning for deceased eminences), follow Bourdieu's and Ermakoff's pattern. Historically this strategy, which I suggest has now been challenged by the emergence of quality genre film, has promoted a disconnection of the Spanish public from a dispossessed and maladjusted film establishment.

Televisual Cinema?

In what remains of this chapter I will propose a new paradigm for the Spanish audiovisual sector at this time of changing habitus. First, I argue for the salience of a new kind of film hostile to earlier auteur or current "other" cinema, a popular school that is steeped in televisual culture but cannot be reduced to it. Second, I argue for the importance of a new quality television that sets itself apart from ordinary TV through aesthetic and social ambitions that might be called (*pace* the aestheticians) cinematic, but draws still on the specificities of a medium now fortified by its convergence with the internet and social media. I focus in film on the thriller as a relatively rare and problematic genre, and in television drama I concentrate on a (more broadly defined) law and justice genre, which is also little practiced in Spain.

My first text is Urbizu's already mentioned *No habrá paz para los malvados*, a brutally efficient thriller that both swept the boards at the Goyas and attracted a domestic audience of almost seven hundred thousand. When a corrupt cop (José Coronado, veteran of quality TV series such as Tele 5's pioneering *Periodistas* ["Journalists," 1998–2002]) drunkenly shoots three dead in a Madrid nightclub, he sets off a double hunt: his own for the sole witness to his crime and that of a woman judge who takes on the murder investigation.

With its expert suspense and action sequences, *No habrá* might seem to be a fine example of that internationalized production that is content to follow the US lead. But this slick genre film has clear local referents. In an early sequence, Coronado stands in a wasteland in front of the four new skyscrapers that have come to symbolize the unsustainable boom and bust of the Spanish economy. And it is a shock to see an actor warmly remembered as a dashing leading man now so battered and grizzled. Moreover, halfway through the film, the thriller veers into politics as the criminal cop blunders into the preparations for an Islamist terror atrocity similar to the one that struck Madrid in 2004.

In an interview at Madrid de Cine, Coronado noted the close connection between the three media of film, television, and theater across which jobbing actors now move at will. Likewise Urbizu's practice shows that skilled directors can make apparently abstract genre films that draw on a US TV aesthetic and yet connect closely with the concerns of local cinema audiences: one actor noted, also at the Screenings, that the film's title had been borrowed for placards in street demonstrations during the continuing economic crisis. Genre cinema thus proves to be an invaluable means for addressing urgent sociopolitical concerns as it moves upmarket and embraces quality scripting, performance, and cinematography.

Following this template, three years later *El niño* (Daniel Monzón, 2011) combined Goya-winning technique (for both special effects and sound) with genre conventions. This drug-smuggling thriller thus boasts big-budget action, beginning in medias res with a taut chase sequence and indulging throughout in frequent helicopter and boat pursuits set and shot in the picturesque Straits of Gibraltar. Newcomer Jesús Castro as the titular youth who will become initiated into narcotics trafficking across the watery border is presented unapologetically for our visual pleasure. This is especially true of a skinny-dipping sequence that the neophyte actor repeatedly claimed in interviews to be especially trying. Confirming this appeal to facile visual pleasure at the expense of more challenging subject matter, the young Spaniard's cross-cultural romance with a young Moroccan woman is sketchily and unconvincingly depicted.

It is precisely through casting, however, that *El niño* establishes its claim, beyond the genre limitations of popular cinema, to quality. Castro is paired with gruff Luis Tosar as his police nemesis, a consecrated actor trailing Goya wins not least as star of prison drama *Celda 211* ("Cell 211," 2009), the previous feature from director Daniel Monzón. Likewise a pliant press stressed the lengthy preparation time spent in preproduction (some five years), a labor intended to serve as guarantor of the second movie's cultural capital. *El País* even praised the character development displayed by Tosar's clichéd troubled police officer (Ordoñez 2015), appealing to a psychological complexity that, beyond the dynamic plotting of the thriller, is often held to be a criterion for artistic quality in cinema.

Yet, striking a balance with the rival television medium, Jesús Castro would later be cast in the second season of Tele 5's police drama *El Príncipe*. And in fact, as we shall see, the latter's first season had fully anticipated the feature film in both its North African setting and focus on geopolitical tensions between Spain and Morocco. Highly accessible and pleasurable, then, *El niño* is an extreme case of my new paradigm: a popular genre film that engages newly emergent mechanisms of legitimation to achieve a degree of that cultural distinction once reserved for auteur or "other" cinema.

El niño was swiftly followed in theatrical release and critical consecration by serial killer movie *La isla mínima* ("Marshland," 2014) directed by Alberto Rodríguez, hitherto known for youth films sometimes starring Spanish television's biggest crossover star, Mario Casas (*7 vírgenes* ["7 Virgins," 2005], *Grupo 7* ["Unit 7," 2012]), to whom I return in the next and final chapter of this book. As period fiction is ubiquitous on television but relatively rare in a feature sector where budgets are now reduced by the crisis, *La isla mínima*'s setting in the Transition to democracy already engages a televisual register. TVE's storied *Cuéntame* has explored the period for over a decade; and Antena 3's *La chica de ayer* ("Yesterday's Girl," 2009) had been a time-traveling police drama set in the same post-Franco era. Moreover, corrupt cop Javier Gutiérrez had been intimately known to Spanish audiences over the preceding five years as the sidekick in TVE's highest-rated series, the already mentioned period romance *Águila roja*.

Beyond format and casting, the serial killer genre, rarer of course in Spain than in the United States, is indigenized here by its placing in a precise temporal and spatial context that owes much to television's perceived closeness to a local audience. Gutiérrez's character is thus not simply a bent cop whose conduct of a multiple murder case of young women is not to be trusted; he is also a veteran of the Francoist security forces who, it is revealed, took part in extrajudicial killings.

Furthermore, as in *El niño*, a transnational-style criminal plot is transformed through a distinctive Andalusian location, in this case the treacherous and picturesque marshland of Doñana. Frequent aerial shots of this distinctive landscape, with its intricately geometric patterns of land and water, are used both for aesthetic effect (the film won the Goya for best cinematography once more) and narrative function (the placing of lost characters in an extreme and disorientating environment). The film uses this very precise setting as part of a general critique of the Transition in an invocation of historical memory that would be amenable to Left-leaning and telephobic tastemakers at newspapers such as *El País*. Indeed in a reality effect that reinforces *La isla mínima*'s expert recreation of the period through production design, the opening credits show documentary footage of the time.

Yet the casting once more of *niño du jour* Jesús Castro in a sinister costar role distances *La isla mínima* once more from the past practices of period filmmaking now identified with a dispossessed and maladjusted film establishment. The presence of new intermediatic star Castro, plus his fellow TV-recognizable cast, thus reconfirms *La isla mínima*'s clear connection with my new paradigm of audience-friendly, but expertly realized, genre cinema.

In these thrillers, then, the televisual mode is engaged in part through the familiarity of the actors, who serve to domesticate a somewhat distant Hollywood genre. But these features remain cinematic in the tensions they display between their generic constraints and their continued aspiration to aesthetic and thematic ambition. As we shall now see, the same perilous equilibrium is seen in three recent television series that fall broadly into the law and justice genre, one of which is as problematic in Spanish TV as it is in Spanish cinema. Here so-called cinematic television (the label applied to special or event programming) takes over the aspiration to national narrative once embodied by auteur cinema without abandoning the seriality that is the defining characteristic of long-form TV drama.

Cinematic TV?

Educated Spaniards would no doubt be surprised to learn that my first example of quality television is Antena 3's drug-dealing drama *Sin tetas no hay paraíso* ("You Don't Get to Heaven Without Tits," 2008–9), a rare Spanish adaptation of a Colombian original. After all, Latin American *telenovela*, which was once widely shown in Spain, is now spurned by critics and audiences alike as a low quality import. Inspired no doubt by the knowingly salacious title (and sometimes showing little knowledge of the actual content of the series that ran for three seasons between 2008 and 2009), politicians and academics alike have attacked the show for its supposed reactionary ideology. Thus we are told that it imposed impossible standards of female beauty, promoted the desirability of violent crime and sex, and reduced women, mesmerized by fatally attractive gangster lovers, to Cinderella-style passivity.

Yet, significantly enough, the changes made by the producers to the original Colombian format reveal Spanish television's new aspirations to psychological and narrative complexity. The main plotline remains teenage Catalina's relationship with the criminal kingpin known as El Duque. But the complication here is that she is in love with him and he treats her tenderly, among other things opposing her desire for the breast implants referred to in the series title. (Conversely the Colombian series begins with a brutally pragmatic episode in which the young heroine fails to the make the grade as a prostitute because of her deficient cup size.) Indeed in the star-making role for Miguel Ángel Silvestre as El Duque, his oft-displayed physique, warmly appreciated by female fans, displaces female anatomy as a source of visual pleasure for the viewer.

Unexpectedly, once more Antena 3's adapters set this central and newly romantic story amid multiple new plot strands that complement and complicate its meaning. Thus they invent a police inspector who is obsessed with taking down the seductive narco *capo* but serves as a problematic embodiment of the law in that he is himself addicted to prescription drugs. Catalina's family, now elevated to lower middle class from the humble deprivation they endured in Colombia, includes a single mother whose tentative romance with a factory owner (played by distinguished film veteran Fernando Guillén Cuervo) provides as reciprocal and respectful a version of heterosexual romance as any feminist academic could hope for. El Duque's conflict with the incoming Colombian narcos who call him "españolito" gives rise to uncommon reflections on a crisis-ridden Spain's newly submissive relationship with Latin America.

Beyond these narrative and thematic complexities, technical credits are also high. There are frequent well-chosen exteriors, placing a transnational plot within a recognizable Madrid setting. For example, the lovers meet in the Parque de Occidente with the Palacio Real standing proudly behind them or enjoy a hotel room with an ominous view of the hulking Telefónica tower on the city skyline outside. When El Duque is forced to flee his home territory, three episodes are even set and shot in the Colombia that remains exotic to Spanish viewers.

Yet the Madrid locations also suggest that the series, in spite of its cinematic complexity and scope, aims for televisual closeness and domesticity. After a difficult day, Catalina makes her daughter a "Spanish omelet," national comfort food. Fans proudly recognize the actress who plays Catalina's frenemy Yéssica (who grooms her young classmates as precocious prostitutes) as a Galician, just like them (María Castro would later go on to play the more sympathetic protagonist of *Vive cantando*, studied in chapter 6). Silvestre, for his part, fielding obtrusive enquiries about his physique and nude scenes to the Spanish press (as *niño* Jesús Castro was later to do), invokes his own workaday origins in Valencia. The production and reception of this show, then, are fully indigenized in a way attempted by the localizing thrillers I studied in the first half of this chapter, but *Sin tetas no hay paraíso* was able to extend deeper and longer into audience affections over three top-rated seasons.

Sin tetas's feminization of the audience is reinforced in a very different example of quality TV, *El tiempo entre costuras* ("The Time in Between," 2013). Invoking the miniseries that is for Buonanno the epitome of European-style authoritative canons of quality, this period romance, a literary adaptation, ran for just eleven feature-length episodes. And exploiting the convergence of film and TV aesthetics, it offered some of the most glamorous and intensely pleasurable visuals ever seen in Spain, whether on big screen or small.

El tiempo entre costuras is a big-budget historical drama about a seamstress-cum-spy. Although broadcast by Antena 3 once more, it is made by Boomerang, an independent production company less known than its rivals, but more versatile. Initially, a period piece may not seem so novel. Antena 3's schedule is itself awash in costume drama with daily serials *Amar es para siempre* ("To Love Is Forever," 2005–) and *El secreto de Puente Viejo* ("The Secret of Puente Viejo," 2011–) occupying some three hours each afternoon in the post-lunch *sobremesa* slot. In their quest for event programming, however, so alien to the daily rhythm of soap and *telenovela*, Antena 3 kept their prestige serial under wraps for almost twelve months, waiting for the right date and building anticipation. The broadcaster was rewarded with an extraordinary rating, averaging 5 million viewers and a 25.3 percent share over the course of the series.

Illustration 8.1: *El tiempo entre costuras* ("The Time in Between," Antena 3, 2013)

The key innovation (and attraction) of *El tiempo entre costuras* is that it is quite literally a costume drama. Initially alone and unaided, Sira, the protagonist, comes to run the most fashionable dressmaking studio in her native Madrid, where she has moved after a period in Morocco. Much action in later episodes takes place in Lisbon, where she seduces a businessman in league with the Nazis. Her true love, however, is a freedom fighter whom she pretends to disdain in order to protect his life. But more frequent and dramatic scenes show the normally self-controlled Sira hugging and sobbing with a female English friend ("Love hurts, darling!").

As Sira sacrifices her relationships with her lover and long-lost father to her somewhat mysterious espionage mission, it might appear that the series is simply a remake of the Hollywood woman's movie: she is a Mildred Pierce who has swapped a baking dish for a sewing machine. The theme of the absent father and uncertain paternity seems similarly taken straight from a Latin American *telenovela*, even though that genre is, as mentioned earlier, no longer successful in Spain.

However, three elements move *El tiempo* on to a different level. The first is the extraordinary care given to mise-en-scène. Every shot is perfectly composed and curated, from (of course) the parade of exquisite costumes to the luxurious authentic locations. Even when Sira is forced to waylay a chicken truck for a secret mission (her pencil skirt means she needs to be carried on board in the driver's arms), she drapes her hair in a cerise chiffon scarf. But given the fact that the narrative focuses precisely on fashion as women's work and feminine guiles (Nazi ladies also come into Sira's orbit drawn by her unparalleled skill with a needle), the extravagant display of wardrobe, apparently incongruous in the context of war-torn Europe, is thematized and does not feel superfluous to the plot.

A second related element after the sumptuous look is the performance by star Adriana Ugarte, who is perfectly (and differently) coiffed and attired in each scene. As we have seen in the case of *Sin tetas*, Spanish series are normally ensemble by nature. It is thus highly unusual that one actor should carry a whole drama on her elegantly clad shoulders. Moreover, Ugarte, who is in almost every shot, gives a highly controlled performance that could not be further from the melodramatics of classic Hollywood or modern *telenovelas*. She brings a sobriety and intensity to a potentially soapy plot whose distinction is intensified by the remarkably leisurely pace of a narrative that seems (like Sira herself) somehow suspended in time.

This brings us to the final characteristic of the show: its relation to history. The grand narrative of the Civil War and Nazism is glimpsed only tangentially through costume, women's work (which comes down to the same thing here), and female psychology, both individual and collective (Sira gathers a crowd of faithful followers at her studio). In spite of this indirect engagement with historical context, then, *El tiempo entre costuras* could be read as a revival of Spain's miniseries of the 1970s and 1980s, which were invariably literary adaptations of the classics. Like, say, TVE's *Fortunata y Jacinta*, *El tiempo* boasts unusually high production values, which are (as mentioned earlier) currently inaccessible to Spanish directors in feature film, whose budgets have (as also mentioned earlier) been cut with the crisis.

The ample Antena 3 budget transforms everyday television into an aesthetic object offering intense visual pleasure. But where the classic serials of the Transition served (as Palacio has shown) to educate Spaniards in the new responsibilities of democracy, the moral of *El tiempo* is more diffuse and private, focusing as it does on female self-realization, both emotional and economic. *El tiempo* thus bids for a quality demographic, which, unlike the family audience still sought by most Spanish series, coincides with the tastes of adult, childless, and professional women. It is telling that after Sira suffers a miscarriage she is not tempted to have another child.

In the same year as Antena 3's *El tiempo*, Tele 5 broadcast expert police series *El Príncipe*, also set in North Africa, in this case the Spanish enclave of Ceuta. *El Príncipe*, named for a real-life neighborhood, engages not only with the drug dealing we saw in *Sin tetas* but also (and I believe this is unprecedented) with Islamist terrorism. And the casting of José Coronado as a corrupt cop means that he brings with him memories of his very similar role in feature film *No habrá paz*. Yet *El Príncipe* also stages a complex and involving love affair between another Christian cop (who is in fact an undercover secret agent, played by Álex González) and a Muslim teacher (Hiba Abouk), the first time that a Spanish actor of Arab descent had been offered an above-the-title role in a TV series or indeed film. This theme is explored at once more subtly and sexily than in the similar thriller *El niño*, which was released after *El Príncipe*'s first season was shown.

By dealing with one of the most charged topics in contemporary Spanish politics and society, jihadism and the relation with a Muslim minority little represented in the media, *El Príncipe* clearly aspired to the status of national narrative. And its aesthetics are also of the highest quality. Rather than shoot on (dangerous) site, the production team employed the Digital Backlot supplied by Stargate Studios, known for quality US shows *Mad Men* and *The Walking Dead*, and used, it was claimed, for the first time in Europe. The high-speed car chase sequence with which the first episode opens would not be envied by *El niño*. And the labyrinthine plot, with its expert cliffhangers and reversals, is based on a script that, rarely in Spain, was preconceived as an artistic whole, one in which every beat is perfectly placed.

Yet it is precisely at this point that *El Príncipe*, an ostentatious example of cinematic TV in its aesthetic, is most televisual. Its narrative effect depends wholly on the seriality of long-form television and its emotional payoff on viewers' continuing cohabitation with its characters (some of the most sympathetic of whom turn out to be terrorists). Indeed the series' density makes the subsequent feature *El niño* feel shallow and hollow ("child's play," perhaps) by comparison. And *El Príncipe*'s meditation on cross-cultural romance (and violence) charts the complexities of both in a way no Spanish film has to date.

It was in the wake of *El Príncipe* that Tele 5 squandered their newly acquired prestige by sending to Morocco, in the footsteps of their prize-winning fictional police officers, despised reality star Belén Esteban. It might appear, then, that each medium will return to its own level. Yet I have argued that, in this new media paradigm for Spain, the emergent genre cinema also appeals to the televisual virtues of closeness or locality in order to indigenize the foreign genre of the thriller; and, that when viewed on a widescreen TV, the aesthetics of the features and series I have treated fully converge. It is significant that after *La isla mínima* triumphed at the Goyas its producer, Mikel Lejarza, described his company Atresmedia (parent company of Antena 3) as a "group committed to cultural creation" and to "the management of audiovisual content" (in general) for an audience that he had no hesitation in calling "intelligent" (Premios Goya 2015).

Spanish television drama has thus achieved a distinctive brand of quality that hybridizes Buonanno's European virtue of cultural respectability (seen in *El tiempo*) with the more novel and edgy American tone (seen in *El Príncipe*), both of which seem to resonate with viewers. And after the problematic period I cited via Madrid de Cine at the start of this chapter, Spanish cinema also achieved a historically high market share in its home market in 2014, due in part to the last two films I examine here. More surprisingly yet, the press, including *El País*, celebrated their genre status as thrillers, praising both the commercial and the artistic success of the year's cinema (Ordoñez 2015).

But I would suggest, finally, that, rejecting the dispossession and maladjustment of the film establishment as they have in the appreciation of an expert popular cinema, viewers and scholars of Spanish media should also pay closer attention to current TV series: expertly crafted national narratives that attract audiences larger and longer lasting than any feature film.

CHAPTER 9

Crisis Fictions
Novel, Cinema, TV

Path Dependence and Desire Lines

Between 2010 and 2012 *El País* published three articles on the current state of three media. First came a debate among what the newspaper called "narrators without limits" (well-known novelists Javier Cercas, Agustín Fernández Mallo, and Almudena Grandes), which ran under a headline that suggested multiple, maritime voyages: "contemporary Spanish narrative and its [nautical] courses (*derroteros*)" (Manrique Sabogal and Rodríguez Marcos 2010). The three novelists, who describe themselves as "writers who belong to a language, not a country," offer a genealogy of the novel in the post-Franco period (in the three stages of experimental, traditional, and personal), identify two indispensable relationships for the modern Spanish novel (with Latin America and with audiovisual culture), and speak of the connection with a reading public that is now difficult to locate in these new times of media transformation and generic fusion "with no geographic or literary limits."

A second article from 2011 recounts the recent history of Spanish cinema in the institutional context of the twenty-fifth anniversary of the Goya awards, relying once more on the suggestive term "courses" or "derroteros" (Fernández Santos 2011). This survey is less positive, alluding as it does to the title of the film that first won the award: *El viaje a ninguna parte* ("Journey to Nowhere," 1986). The journalist emphasizes the fraught relationship between the government and the creative and commercial professionals it sponsors ("the restructuring of the financial system which supports [the film industry] like a chronically sick patient") and the currently negative attitude toward Spanish films by audiences in theaters ("the worst connection with the public in the history of Spanish film"). Ironically, then, while Spanish cinema has globalized (turning itself into "a luxurious shop window for international stars" such as Almodóvar and his favored actors), it has succeeded in provoking only "scorn" in its local audience. As it "goes through one of its most critical transitions," Spanish film is now dependent on television (the most popular star is Mario Casas, who combines TV series with teen movies) and is "polarized" between superproductions, often shot in English, and microbudget films whose distribution is highly restricted. Spanish cinema, which we are told "was always in crisis," now confronts "the perfect storm."

Finally, *El País* published a general article on television (Marcos 2012), one of several on the changing fortunes of the medium to suggest that "if Shakespeare were alive today" he would be writing for TV. According to the journalist, the current "Golden Age" of TV series has transformed a genre once thought to be minor, revealing its unique strengths such as the possibility of developing a complex narrative and contradictory characters over many hours. As is common in Spanish coverage of the medium, this article cites only examples from the United States; and indeed it echoes commentaries on the new status of television previously made in the *New York Times*.

But Spanish specialist sources cited in the article are more flexible. Antonio Muñoz Carrión, a professor of communication studies, stresses the functionalism of the category of aesthetics, saying that "for something to be considered art, it requires only a generalized belief in its artistic value." Pedro Pérez, then president of FAPAE, cites instead transformations in habits of consumption: "More than film and television changing, what has changed is people's behavior and their allocation of leisure time."

This article thus suggests the possibility of a tectonic change in the status of the three media I discuss in this final chapter: television drama, in certain cases at least, outstrips not just cinema but also the novel in its artistic ambition and social reach. Given the persistence in Spain of the rhetoric of *telebasura* (trash TV), which originated in the Transition to democracy and remains hostile to any serious consideration of the medium, this trend would suggest a transformation of the mechanisms of legitimation that structure the cultural field in general.

The context of these journalistic debates is of course the crisis (at once economic, political, and social) that has shaken the Spanish state since 2007 and has changed Spaniards' image of themselves (I have examined the real estate dimension of this crisis in chapter 6 of this book.) Novelist Cercas suggests in the first article that, compared to Latin America, Spain is "very tiny" ("una cosa muy pequeñita"). Film directors, generally identified with the Left, attack the reduction in government support and the increase in sales tax on movie tickets. Even in the television sector, more profitable and less reliant on the state, professionals claim budget cuts have threatened respected series on public broadcaster TVE, while one minister's claim that such series are just a way of "passing the time" offended all in the industry.

Beyond such specific statements, I would like to propose in this chapter a general working hypothesis that will not seem implausible in such extreme times: namely that there has emerged in Spain a fiction (or fictions) of the crisis that is expressed across various media. Two preliminary questions arise. First, what are the aesthetic and narrative characteristics of this fiction? And second, how does the expression of the crisis vary from novel to film to television? Given the different positions still occupied by these media in the Spanish cultural field, sketched out above, the forms of my hypothetical crisis fiction are likely to be varied.

The best-known Greek-English dictionary (Lyddell-Scott-Jones 2015) defines the word "crisis" in a wide range of contexts. Fundamentally meaning "separation" or "distinction," it can further be used to name a juridical verdict, a case that can be decided only by war, or a turning point in the development of a disease. These definitions suggest that, beyond specific contexts that are legal, military, or medical, a crisis will be unexpected, uncertain, and threatening but can take place only within a complex system, such as cultural production and reception.

If we analyze a textual corpus in Spain produced in recent years across different media, we note two broad patterns. On the one hand there is a strong trend toward historical texts, period fictions that explore the Spanish past from the Roman era to the Transition to democracy and beyond. On the other hand (and these works are less numerous but more striking), there is a body of fantastic fiction, which seems to turn its back on a contemporary reality that is too painful for the audience. Clearly the first tendency has received much more attention from Hispanists, concerned as they have been with the historical memory of the Francoist regime within the current democracy and appealing as they often do to psychoanalytic paradigms such as the return of the repressed. The fantastic genre has received less attention from scholars, although David Roas leads a pioneering project on the subject at Barcelona's Autonomous University. But while it is evident that both trends can be read as an escape from the painful current crisis, both also refer obliquely to topical issues, albeit placed in an unfamiliar context, in an attempt to engage the contemporary audience. In this chapter I focus on the less-studied fantasy narratives.

As we shall see, one notable feature of my corpus of crisis fictions is that they appeal to a privileged location: the enclosed space or, more particularly, the prison. Moreover, when reference is made to open and ample spaces (for example the desert or ocean), they tend to be barren and threatening locations. In crisis fictions every journey leads nowhere and every street comes to a dead end. Moreover, while the enclosed space can be read as either womb or tomb, the open space no long means liberty but rather the lack of any human presence.

To engage with this emerging corpus of crisis fiction we need an approach that can tackle both the external (institutional) aspects of cultural objects and their internal (textual) qualities. We might appeal to the field theory of Bourdieu, the postmodernism of Lyotard, or the less-known area of intermediality. And I will make some reference to each of these approaches. But what I prefer in this chapter is to try out a new model of cultural creativity that derives from economics and cultural geography. The key terms in this analysis will be "path dependency" and "desire lines." Before turning to my chosen specimen texts I will sketch out these concepts, which are fundamental to my analysis and surely less known than the other approaches mentioned above. In general terms my approach will be based more on space than time, more on topography than chronology.

The best known example of path dependency remains the QWERTY keyboard. Designed in the nineteenth century as a response to the limits of the typewriters of the time, this arbitrary organization of the alphabet has survived until our own internet era. The constant motto in definitions of path dependency is, thus, the following: "History matters" (*Economist* 2013; Magnusson 2009). In 2012 alone, the *Economist* used the term in analyses of topics as diverse as electric cars, the reform of US health care, light bulbs, and alternative technologies. An example of my own that comes closer to home for this chapter is the distribution of public funds for film production in Spain. Favoring as it does established professional incumbents, such funding often fails to take account of the current configuration of the audience to whom such films are supposedly addressed.

Conversely, in spite of the long and heavy inheritance of path dependency (a concept not unrelated to Bourdieu's "habitus"), there exists the further term of "emergence," also used in a wide variety of sociological and economic contexts. The qualities of emergence (the origin of novelty, creativity, and authorship) cannot be reduced to the constitutive elements of their original system and exhibit interconnectivity and unintended consequences (Holland 2000). New and complex phenomena can thus arise from multiple, simple interactions.

The most everyday (and yet the most poetic) example of emergence is the desire line. This is an anonymous and collective path in a public space that occurs when official routes (inheritors of the well-named "path dependency") no longer serve the individuals for whom they were devised. Desire lines, fragile traces made in grass or even snow, tend to be shortcuts, following the shortest distance between two points. But a glance at the photo collection of the same name on Flickr reveals that they can also be curved, multiple, or bifurcated. Ephemeral as they are, desire lines reveal nonetheless the traces of the physical trajectories of unknown walkers, authentic pioneers of urban emergence (Murray 2007).

What I shall suggest in the rest of this chapter is that some contemporary Spanish narrators in novel, film, and television, who are necessarily dependent on the institutional paths that precede them, have been able nonetheless (and sometimes in collaboration with an anonymous public) to produce new and creative desire lines.

Tracking the Novel: Agustín Fernández Mallo

Nocilla Lab, the third novel in a trilogy, was launched in Barcelona's FNAC bookstore in 2009 with the following words: "This is the culmination of the literary project that has shaken up the literary scene in Spanish" (Alfaguara 2009). The multinational publishing house Alfaguara tempted the audience by promising a multimedia "session of video, music, and text … which is fragmented and contemporary, pixelated and appropriated, [and] whose guiding threads are the theory of the image, contemporary poetry, the consumer society, and the novel *Nocilla Lab*."

Given these grand ambitions, satirized in the novel itself in its frequent reference to the mysterious "Project" undertaken by the protagonist and his girlfriend, Fernández Mallo would seem to be identified with those "writers without limits" cited in *El País*. Moreover, carefully cosmopolitan, he also presents himself as a writer who belongs to a language (Spanish) not a country (Spain). The literary citations most evident in his novel will thus be to two Latin American masters of the fantastic genre, Borges and Cortázar. A quote from the latter's story *Casa tomada*, an illustrious antecedent in literary claustrophobia, will serve as an epigraph to *Nocilla Lab*.

Experimental in his technique and personal in his subject matter (the self-named narrator replays autobiographical episodes of the author's life), Fernández

Mallo displays a consistent engagement with audiovisual media (the trilogy is supplemented by a medium-length film posted on the web) and with his readership (although little active on Twitter, he hosts a long-lasting blog that allows contact with fans whom he also encounters in live performances). And if crisis is, etymologically, separation or distinction, then the Nocilla trilogy has provoked dramas in the legal sphere (the author was sued for plagiarism by the Borges estate), the military (the novel makes some problematic references to the fall of the Twin Towers), and the medical community (the source of the trilogy is a traffic accident that confined its author to a hotel room in Thailand).

Fernández Mallo's work also signals a crisis in the Spanish literary field. Initially published by the small press Candaya, he managed to make his presence felt and achieve a critical and popular acclaim that were by no means inevitable. Vincent Moreno has written an excellent article along these lines showing, in Bourdieu's terms, how Fernández Mallo succeeded in changing the habitus of contemporary narrative in spite (or because) of the fact that he occupied an initially marginal position that rendered much more difficult his quest for the symbolic capital that is both the effect and instrument of cultural distinction (2012, 88).

It is not the least of Fernández Mallo's achievements, then, that he has become the most representative of modern novelists while displaying postmodern attitudes that are generally not favored by Spanish critics. These are a skepticism toward politics and history (here the narrator looks in vain for TV listings in the Marxist daily *Mundo Obrero* ["Workers' World"] [2009a, Kindle location 173]), a love of hybridity (the novel juxtaposes Cortázar and Coca-Cola, theoretical physics and Andy Warhol), and consumerist frivolity (the Spanish version of Nutella that generously lent its brand name to the trilogy). And while Fernández Mallo's narrative is ambitiously transmedial (embracing as it does print, comic, video, and internet), the Project within the novel is presented as a failure, albeit a highly conscious one. *Nocilla Lab* is a road movie (the English phrase recurs in the novel) set on an anonymous island south of Sardinia that concludes in a dead end: a prison converted into an unlikely hotel. The impressive emergence of a new form of Spanish narrative is thus combined with the intense sensation of claustrophobia that is so characteristic of our crisis fictions.

In fact, and in spite of this will to nomadism or Situationist *dérive* "with no route map at all" (2009a, 307), all of the locations in the novel become as enclosed as the Thai hotel room "where my life was reduced to a bed ... and a remote control" (2009a, 240). And although the protagonist first styles himself "the captain of the ship" (the car in which he is driving with his partner [2009a, 321]), soon he will run into a disturbing remnant of the history of this barren place, a ruined building with the sign: "State Recreational Center. Year of Fascism 1938" (334).

In spite of critics' interest in the internet in Fernández Mallo's work, the ubiquitous medium in his trilogy is in fact television. The main character's student life is fed with coffee, a typewriter, and "two television sets" (2009a, 656). When he is imprisoned in the rural tourist site, he scribbles on photos taken of his TV or even fries eggs on its warm screen (2009a, 1763). Moving beyond the dismissal of mass media so frequent in Spain, television is for Fernández Mallo an essential condition of existence on a fantastic island that is the product of an obscure catastrophe, so appropriate for these times of crisis.

The novel's last location is thus at once the most marked by political history and the most fantastic: the prison that has been converted into tourist accommodation and is compared to "a piece of an ocean liner beached in a dried up sea" (2009a, 1478). As much as his physical confinement, the pressure of the tradition of fantastic literature in Spanish weighs heavily on an author who constantly reminds us of his path dependency: the debt to past masters Borges and Cortázar. This is especially true of the climax in which one "Agustín Fernández Mallo" meets another in the prison and kills him with a knife.

Within the diagesis, then, *Nocilla Lab* is a journey to nowhere or, in its own words, "a dead end street" (2009a, 938). But I would like to suggest that outside it, Fernández Mallo's creative innovation is a clear example of a desire line, traced by the author along with collaborators named and unnamed. It is striking that the mid-length video posted on his blog, which is parallel to the print trilogy, shows repeated scenes of the author running in urban or desert landscapes, creating a path as he does so (Fernández Mallo 2009b). We even glimpse in the film an exemplary work by British land artist Richard Long, a photograph of the performance piece called "A Line Made by Walking." It shows an ephemeral trace in the grass that became a seminal piece in the international conceptual art so well known to Fernández Mallo.

Nocilla Lab concludes with the twin murder-suicide of the two Fernández Mallos, an act celebrated (how else?) with what the novel calls "a last Coca Cola" (2009a, 1940). This showy disappearance of the first-person protagonist is accompanied nonetheless, as we have seen, by an equally emphatic extension of the author's brand into the cultural field. Hence, through his transmedia practice, Fernández Mallo has demonstrated to his readers a way in which new and complex systems ("Projects," with a capital P) can emerge from multiple, tiny interactions. They thus form cultural objects (such as his novel and film) that cannot be reduced to their constitutive parts, however recognizable those parts may be.

Scarring Film: Pedro Almodóvar

Pedro Almodóvar wrote in his 'Director's Notes' to his eighteenth feature *La piel que habito* ("The Skin I Live In"), which premiered in 2012, "There are irreversible processes, paths without return, journeys that go only one way. Against her will the protagonist travels one of these paths, is violently obliged to undertake a journey from which she cannot return" (Almodóvar 2011). This commentary is a verdict on the story of Víctor/Vera (Jan Cornet/Elena Anaya), the victim of a forced sex change at the hands of the obsessive surgeon Ledgard, played by Antonio Banderas. But it is also a very apt image for the course ("derrotero") of the auteur of the film, who seems with this work forced to tread once again the same cinematic path.

At a time when Spanish cinema resembled more and more a chronically sick patient kept alive by government finance, the productions of El Deseo (the Almodóvar brothers' company) did not depend on public funding. At the Spanish Film Screenings, the media market that I attended in Madrid in 2012 (as mentioned in the previous chapter), Agustín proudly stated that his film was produced without a euro of state support. And while the presence of Banderas, recently returned from Hollywood, suggested perhaps the luxurious cinematic "shop window" of international stars criticized by *El País*, the film, taking a relatively modest middle path, avoided that polarization between superproductions, often shot in English, and low-budget, badly distributed indies.

Once more at the Screenings, Agustín criticized Spanish producers' attempts to compete with Hollywood by backing projects that starred Anglo-American actors and lacked any connection with "Spanish cultural values." Holding fast to these national marks of identity was, he said, how El Deseo had survived the current crisis, as it had others. It was perhaps ironic, then, that Agustín, spokesperson of a certain cultural nationalism, accepted in this forum the prize for the Spanish feature with the highest international profile: *La piel*, he said, had been sold to forty-two countries and been seen by 4.2 million spectators. The Almodóvar brothers did thus coincide with the newly global routes of Spanish cinema, which, as also mentioned in the previous chapter, grossed twice as much outside its home country than within it. Their film itself obliquely acknowledged this transnational awareness through the presence of a tiger-dressed Brazilian, a refugee from the carnival, whose animal sensuality was somewhat clichéd.

Though feted by both the industry and the foreign press, Almodóvar held no more secure a position at home than than he did on the release of *Los abrazos rotos* in 2009. Acclaimed in Cannes, *La piel* was, once more, harshly criticized by some Spanish journalists. And if Almodóvar has not definitively acquired the distinction described by Bourdieu, it is because he remains associated by critics with clichés of postmodernism (superficiality, frivolity) that have pursued him since the times of the Madrid *movida*. More relevant to our analysis is perhaps the postmodern condition as described by Lyotard.

La piel ignores the convulsions of the time it was made (it is set in "Toledo, 2012") and seems skeptical of the grand narratives of politics and psychoanalysis. Indeed, by limiting itself to an exclusive moneyed milieu as it does, the film eludes any clear connection with the socioeconomic crisis that shook Spain during its shoot. The luxurious prison to which its main character is confined could hardly be further from the street protests of the *indignados*. Nonetheless I will argue that the film's central motif of skin reveals a commitment to emergence that a more explicit social realism could not have addressed.

What is evident, however, is that, retreading his steps in *La piel*, Almodóvar depends on his own past path. The repetitions are clear: the film's stress on surgical paraphernalia (reminiscent perhaps of the medical definition of "crisis") recalls *Todo sobre mi madre* ("All about My Mother," 1999); Ledgard's voyeurism replays the videotaping of *Kika* (1993), as does an overextended scene of rape; the kidnapping of Elena Anaya recalls that of Victoria Abril in *¡Átame!* ("Tie Me Up! Tie Me Down!," 1992). Even the sequence in which Víctor is hosed down echoes that of Carmen Maura's Tina in *La ley del deseo* ("The Law of Desire," 1987), a film in which Banderas also played an obsessive assassin. The figure of the avenging transgender, central to *La piel*, had already appeared in *La ley* once more and *La mala educación* (2004). It is even included in an unpublished story of the 1970s (Smith 2009b). History, at once personal and cinematic, counts here, transforming the experience of the director's faithful fans and enriching it with memories of a back catalogue shared by cineaste and cinephile over the decades.

Nonetheless, in spite of this path dependency (which depends, it has to be said, on a path that is anomalous and autonomous, compared to the hallowed ways of Spanish cinema), the main motif of *La piel* offers a clear example of new emergence. The surgeon Ledgard pieces together pieces of skin from different sources to create a novel object: the perfect body of Vera, the new woman. Vera herself sews together scraps of cloth to create original fabric dolls, reminiscent of Louise Bourgeois sculptures. And finally Almodóvar himself montages fragments of his earlier works to make a new film whose main characteristics (cruelty, darkness, fantasy) are unprecedented in his corpus. Moreover, gender reassignment (a theme especially associated with Almodóvar), once liberating, is here for the first time tragic, a dead end for an artificial creation whose name ("Vera") could not be more ironic. It is striking also that although *La piel* is based on a novel (the French *Mygale* by Thierry Jonquet), Almodóvar is flagrantly unfaithful to his source. The most striking elements of the film's plot (the backstory of Marisa Paredes's character and the unnerving tiger-man, who is revealed as Paredes's daughter and Ledgard's stepbrother) do not appear in the novel.

What *La piel* has in common with the other crisis fictions discussed in this chapter (beyond the theme of the prison, so emphatic here) is transmedia, most especially television. As already noted, Ledgard views his victim via video camera and is obsessed with her image on screen. The security camera is the only access to this prison-like home and the TV screen the only contact the prisoner has with the outside world. Covertly citing fantasy fiction on television, Almodóvar cast as Ledgard's traumatized daughter Blanca Suárez, a young actor then known for her fantasy series for Antena 3: *El internado* ("The Boarding School," 2007–10) and (as we shall see) *El barco* ("The Boat," 2011–13).

When he presented his film to the New York press at Lincoln Center, Almodóvar stated emphatically that Víctor/Vera is at all times conscious of his male identity and never wavers in it. The director even claimed that he himself knows what the difference is between male and female subjects. Such a statement flies in the face of the superficiality and transitivity (the popular understanding of postmodernism) associated with Almodóvar for so long. And there seems no doubt that the austere Vera has little in common with the outrageous Tina of *La ley del deseo*, a character with whom she shares nonetheless a sex change and a frustrated love life. Treading like his characters a hitherto unknown desire line, just like the surgeon leaves scars time and again on the skin of his victim, Almodóvar has created in *La piel* a perfect film for the uncertain times of crisis: a cinematic trail made up of multiple elements and inducing menacing effects.

Televisual Routes: *El barco*

The curious coincidence of the time of crisis and the golden age of television suggests that TV series have not been as affected as novels and films by the unexpected transformation of the socioeconomic field in Spain. Unlike much feature film, television production has been able to connect with its local audience. And if Spanish novelists are seeking to reach an international public, TV creators, narrators without limits, have already done so. Spanish series are successfully exported abroad, either in their original version or as formats to be adapted locally.

Exploiting the development of plots across multiple episodes, current series aspire to the symbolic capital of the nineteenth-century novel, whose form of distribution was so similar in its seriality and periodicity. And combining quality and popularity, the new series transcend the division in the film field between superproductions intended for a mass audience and microbudget art movies destined for a small minority. Nor has the arrival of the new medium of internet weakened TV series in Spain. Rather, as we shall see, taking advantage of the interconnectivity of social media, must-see television has reinforced the conditions of its own consumption.

El barco is a big-budget series shown on private free to air network Antena 3 and made by Spain's most illustrious producer, Globomedia. It is at once the most apocalyptic of our crisis fictions (beginning as it does with the end of the world, no less) and the most profitable. Taking its bow in January 2011 with an audience of almost 5 million (four times the total audience of *La piel*), this was the most successful launch of a local series in the three years since the financial crisis began. Connecting with a general audience, it led in all the age demographics from four to sixty-four.

The official synopsis is as follows:

¿Qué pasaría si de la noche a la mañana nos despertáramos y el mundo no estuviera ahí?, ¿qué pasaría si el fin del mundo te pillara encerrado en un buque-escuela de apenas 50 metros de eslora?, ¿qué pasaría si los únicos habitantes del planeta fueran tus compañeros de tripulación? (FormulaTV 2011a)

What would happen if from one day to the next we woke up to find the world was no longer there? What would happen if the end of the world found you shut up in a training ship just fifty meters long? What would happen if the only people left on the planet were your companions in the crew?

Illustration 9.1: Mario Casas and Blanca Suárez in *El barco* ("The Boat," Antena 3, 2011–13)

This opening premise of *El barco* has some similarities to the fantastic fictions we have already examined in this chapter which preceded it. Like *Nocilla Lab*, a novel rich in maritime metaphors, *El barco* offers isolated and barren locations (a prison-like boat and an empty ocean); and like *La piel* it explores the theme of scientific technology gussied up with fantasy, although here it is not a question of transgenic surgery but of a Swiss particle accelerator (coincidentally, also cited by Fernández Mallo) that causes a black hole that swallows up all the land on earth.

Antena 3's apparently unprecedented series employed cinematic techniques, with many scenes shot expensively on a real boat on the high seas and others on an equally costly life-size set built in a studio. Thus the exaggeration of the opening situation (a perfect storm representing the crisis that left Spaniards all adrift) is mirrored in the heightened and exceptional attention to production values here. Moreover, this apparently very Spanish premise (foreigners are vanishingly scarce on board) worked in a global context: when the third and final season ended in February 2013, it was announced that the series had been seen in more than thirty countries, including sixteen in Latin America (FórmulaTV 2013). The series disproved two clichés about current television: that in a time of fragmentation, there was no more family audience; and that in a time of multimedia, viewers could no longer concentrate on long-form, complex narrative.

Although it seemed so new and thus so appropriate for crisis conditions, *El barco* depended still on a certain televisual path. For example, the main cast constitutes an implicit history of television in Spain. Juanjo Altero, who plays the captain, had been a child star of a legendary series of the Transition, *Verano azul* ("Blue Summer," TVE, 1981–82). Colombian Juan Pablo Shuk (the villain Gamboa) came to fame in 2003 in *Pasión de gavilanes* ("Hawks' Passion"), one of the few Latin American *telenovelas* to leap the scheduling fence into Spanish prime time. Youthful Mario Casas (the rebellious stowaway Ulises) is, as previously mentioned, the most representative figure of the current Spanish audiovisual scene, in that he has starred in box-office-friendly feature films without abandoning the series in which he became a celebrity. In the same way, Blanca Suárez (Ainhoa) had just left Antena 3's previous mystery *El internado* to shoot Almodóvar's *La piel*, in which she played, as in *El barco*, the protagonist's daughter.

The most striking innovation, however, in a Spanish context was the series' engagement with social media. Twitter profiles were created for the ensemble cast and updated during the week as if they were real (this was of course somewhat implausible given the apocalyptic premise of the series). And one hour before each episode was broadcast, a so-called "Twittersode" was launched, using the characters' feeds to construct a narrative complementary to that of the TV series. Fernández Mallo's (and Almodóvar's) timid incursion into the internet with their respective blogs is limited compared to this systematic transmedia interaction employed by a TV fiction in collaboration with its anonymous fans over some three years.

Exploiting this intimate and continuous contact with a general audience, *El barco* turned itself into the most potent allegory of the Spanish crisis. And the story of national history embodied in this emblematic ship of state is interwoven with the individual perspectives of each crew member. For example, in the very first episode the captain states that they will all have to learn to live together and respect each other. His daughter, meanwhile, comments in similar but more literal terms: "We're all in the same boat."

In this discursive context, the distinguishing feature of the series is then not so much the initial catastrophe as the difficulty of solidarity in times when "impossible things are happening." Thus fantastic phenomena (an inexplicable tsunami, a marine monster, a deadly fog) are combined with allegorical plotlines on state governance in an age of crisis. In the third episode the captain resolves not to reveal to the young people the gravity of the situation so as to "maintain normal conditions." But the latter mutiny, insisting on returning to a port that no longer exists. In the sixth episode, the rebel crew demand elections, against the captain's wishes. Comparing his troubles with those of Adolfo Suárez, a president of the Transition, the captain proclaims, "A boat is not a community association," to which the young people reply, "It's not a dictatorship either." The captain will thenceforward be obliged to share his power with the "mayor" Ulises, directly and democratically elected by his fellow *indignados*.

In keeping with a mainstream series that seeks to represent the whole nation, *El barco*'s politics is not always so progressive, however. The main conflict in the show is between the captain (father of Ainhoa) and Ulises (her suitor) with the malevolent Gamboa, who is a rival both for the control of the boat and the affections of the girl. The fact that this black-clad baddy (the rest of the cast wear white in publicity shots) is Latin American is perhaps evidence for a new anxiety of Spain toward the challenges posed by that continent. But a hostility to Europe also makes itself felt: supposedly, the global catastrophe is the fault of shadowy scientists in Geneva, who also figure in flashback to a sinister backstory.

This disturbing xenophobic tendency is reinforced by the conservative conditions experienced in a boat that is virtually subject to curfew. After hesitating for some time, the captain allows a young priest to set up an altar on board and celebrate a mass in which almost all the cast participate, bathed in celestial light. And unlike other teen shows of the same period, *El barco* boasts no LGBT characters. Mario Casas's resourceful Ulises takes on the traditional male role of the daring macho, while Blanca Suárez's Ainhoa is often reduced to watching him, tearfully or adoringly.

Hence the fantasy and political plotlines are combined with romantic episodes that are more typical of Latin American *telenovelas*. All of the boat's unwilling inhabitants, whether adult or adolescent, seem to fall in love at some point, even though they come from broken homes (the captain's wife had died before the first episode). In one episode the youngsters even take part in a session of speed dating. *El barco* thus suggests that even in times of crisis (unexpected, uncertain, and threatening), affects count as much as concrete conditions. But this appeal to emotion, which is conservative insofar as it tends to reconstruct the traditional family unit, is somewhat undermined by the series' flagrant product placement. On internet forums fans mock the lavish supplies of Coca-Cola on the boat, a product that was also a fetish in *Nocilla Lab* (FórmulaTV 2011b). The persistence of capitalism, even after the end of the world, reminds us that the solidarity so trumpeted in *El barco*'s indignant dialogues is no rival for the consumer society that the crew, condemned to a one-way journey, have supposedly left behind.

At one point Ainhoa throws a message in a bottle into the sea. Like the wake of the boat that appears so insistently in publicity shots for the series, the bottle will leave at best a fragile desire line in the postapocalyptic ocean. But because this bottle is, we are told, "the last Coca-Cola in the world" it reveals in spite of itself the necessary complicity between aesthetics and economics in this definitive example of TV crisis fiction.

Path, Scar, Wake

Our three narratives (in novel, cinema, and television) undertake journeys to nowhere: they put into play irreversible processes, paths without return, and one-way trips that end (if they end at all) in enclosed spaces. Perhaps this motif of the prison responds to the feeling that (as one novelist said to *El País*) "Spain is now a very tiny thing." But these crisis fictions also provide evidence of a tension, difficult to resolve, between grand national history and individual, indeed idiosyncratic, perspectives. Thus, if all three works can be read as collective allegories, they are also unrepentantly specific and eccentric in their textual detail and artistic form.

Perhaps the solution to this impasse lies in a return to the philosophical sources of postmodernism: Lyotard confronted the eclipse of the metadiscourses of

Marxism and liberalism with the multiple, tiny voices of the Soviet Gulag. Germán Labrador Méndez has begun microresearch of this kind in a 2012 article called "Las vidas *subprime*: la circulación de *historias de vida* como tecnología de imaginación política en la crisis española" ("Subprime Lives: The Circulation of *Life Stories* as a Technology of Political Imagination in the Spanish Crisis"). While Labrador Méndez explores the real-life tragedies recounted in the nonfiction press, his analysis might be extended, as I have here, to equally resonant and troubling fictional media stories. The latter also suggest a kind of imagination that is necessarily political as well as technological.

I have also suggested here that in these new circumstances television transcends both novel and film in its artistic ambition and social reach. *El barco* succeeded, over its three seasons, in serving as a disturbing metaphor for a crisis that was as extended as it was unexpected. Of course private TV, even when it is free to air as here, cannot be unaffected by the consumer society that is celebrated so ironically by Fernández Mallo in his Nocilla Trilogy. Nonetheless, the television industry has, unlike the less-professionalized cinema sector, been able to navigate with great skill the perfect storm of the crisis. But what I have attempted to show here is how in all three media new and complex fictions can emerge from multiple, small interactions, and that the fragile desire line deserves to be followed in its many forms of Fernández Mallo's path made in the desert, Almodóvar's scars cut in the skin, and *El barco*'s wake traced in a postapocalyptic ocean.

Conclusion
The Audiovisual Field in Contemporary Spain

In the introduction to this book I asked, beyond the pessimism of many of the texts examined here, for readers to be open to a final and more positive moral: the emergence of new and complex cultural phenomena arising from the multiple interactions of transmedia. I hope to have demonstrated the creativity of the audiovisual field in contemporary Spain through the varied textual analyses throughout.

Moreover, beyond the final section of chapters explicitly labeled as "transmedia," we have seen that, as in Agnes Petho's account of "intermediality" discussed in the introduction, Spanish film and television can be read as inherently heterotopic. Thus Spanish cinema of the democratic 1980s, which attempted to reestablish its artistic prestige after the much-scorned popular film of the Dictatorship, was based on literary adaptations and on the incorporation of elements taken from the now ubiquitous medium of television. Conversely, Spanish film production of the 2000s, proudly exhibited to the foreign press at Madrid de Cine, is funded and promoted by multimedia holding companies in which TV networks play the leading role. And Almodóvar, Spain's most painstaking auteur, seeks to craft an artistic persona by way of an internet practice that threatens always to escape his control. Likewise, the television seasons of the Spanish national networks draw on actors already consecrated by cinema or (in the case of Catalonia) producers and politicians alike submit both media to a common program of nation-building and linguistic normalization. Even when television tackles a vital contemporary theme little explored by film (the construction bubble and housing crisis), it does so in greatly different formats (sitcom and drama) and for widely divergent audiences (mass and niche).

Beyond the specific question of intermedia, then, industrial and institutional questions have also been highlighted here. What does it mean for a national cinema to have a larger audience abroad than at home? Can free to air network television be appraised using the same criteria as the subscription cable quality shows that are much rarer in Spain than elsewhere? Does the crossover between the two media, which has been constant for much longer than is commonly supposed, mean that film and TV should no longer be treated analytically as discrete media?

Recent developments have tended to confirm the ambivalent answers already suggested to these questions in the nine preceding chapters. Thus critics in Spain continue to promote a so-called "Other Cinema" of low budgets, minimalist aesthetics, and restricted distribution, a new auteur cinema that has also made its mark abroad ("L'Autre Cinéma Espagnol" was the name of a Parisian festival in June 2015). Yet newly proficient genre films, most recently the romantic comedy *Ahora o nunca* ("Now or Never," María Ripoll, 2015), continue to attract mass local audiences, rivaling the box office of Hollywood blockbusters. In the television sector, the apparently moribund state network TVE most unexpectedly produced the critically and popularly acclaimed science fiction series *El ministerio del tiempo* ("The Ministry of Time," 2015), which I mentioned in the introduction and was nominated as a candidate for the prestigious Prix Europa. This latter title was known for its pioneering transmedia dimension, giving rise to an unprecedented quantity and quality of fan-produced art and text shared on the web among devotees known appositely as *Ministéricos* (a mash-up of "ministry" and "hysterical").

Recent scholars of US media have suggested that the leveling of distinctions and blurring of boundaries inherent in transmedia (most particularly the proliferation of unpaid fan labor on the web that is ambiguously allied to corporate interests) may produce risks as well as to opportunities (Perlman 2015, 174). Contributors to *El ministerio del tiempo*'s highly controlled Whatsapp group were even expelled by the series' creative team if their amateur work was judged to be not up to standard. Yet, in a Spanish context, it would be premature to carry out an ideological critique of an actively creative fandom or consumer culture that is much less developed than in the United States.

As Bourdieu writes in *Distinction*, "Detachment, disinterestedness, indifference—aesthetic theory has so often presented these as the only way to recognize the work of art for what it is ... that one ends up forgetting that they really mean ... the refusal to invest oneself and take things seriously" (2009, 34). The belated blurring of the divide between high and low culture in Spain (the growing appreciation of popular cinema and mass television) reveals that critics and consumers alike are no longer refusing to invest themselves, refusing to take (media) things seriously.

This change testifies to what Bourdieu once more calls the popular "aesthetic": "a deep-rooted demand for participation" in fiction (2009, 32). Yet it is striking that several of the popularly successful texts I have studied (most evidently Almodóvar's *Los abrazos rotos*) combine an invitation to frank emotion with the employment of the techniques of artistic distancing that signal for Bourdieu the "detachment of the aesthete" (2009, 34).

Bourdieu also cites in this context Rousseau's seminal *Lettre à d'Alembert sur les spectacles* (2009, 34), a pamphlet penned against the establishment of a theater in Geneva. Among other claims, the *Lettre* blames vain and vulnerable women spectators for the dangerous immorality of the dramatic spectacle (Rousseau 2015, 31). As in *telenovelas*, the female "realm" is here said to be restricted to love (Rousseau 2015, 23). For Rousseau, even an acknowledged masterpiece such as Molière's *Le Misanthrope* outrages public morality by making mock of a protagonist who, Rousseau claims, seeks only to sagely critique the vices of his time, including the frivolous women of court (Rousseau 2015, 18).

This dismissal of mass culture is still common in elite Spanish circles where jeremiads against the supposed damage wreaked by trashy TV and obsessive internet use remain constant in the press. But this Spanish discourse is, like Rousseau's polemic, also gendered: popular television is held implicitly to be a female spectacle, while the "difficult men" of quality TV drama (parallel to their peers in auteur cinema) are thought to be noble exceptions to the general rule of mass-media degradation.

Yet I have argued that audiovisual fiction in all media can serve as a way of working through social issues and learning about the world, even in comedies less distinguished than those of Molière. Visual and narrative pleasure, now more apparent than ever on a smaller screen that has become bigger in size and scope, need not necessarily be in conflict with this process. Finally, then, Spain offers lessons not just in the creation of films and TV formats that have been exported around the world but also in the configuration of an audiovisual field at home that consistently resists reduction to globalized norms.

Bibliography

Alfaguara. 2009. "Presentación de Nocilla Lab en Madrid." Accessed October 14. http://www.alfaguara.com/es/noticia/presentacion-de-nocilla-lab-en-madrid/.

Almodóvar, Pedro. 2009. "Blog Pedro Almodóvar." Accessed June 12, 2010. http://www.pedroalmodovar.es/.

———. 2011. "*La piel que habito*: notas del director." Accessed September 15, 2012. http://www.lapielquehabito.com/info.php?lang=es.

Amago, Samuel. 2013. *Spanish Cinema in the Global Context*. New York: Routledge.

Anon. 2005. "Almodóvar deja la Academia de Cine en protesta por la votación de los Goya." *El País*, February 7. Accessed June 12, 2010. http://www.elpais.com/articulo/cultura/Almodovar/deja/Academia/Cine/protesta/sistema/votacion/Goya/elpepucul/20050207elpepucul_2/Tes.

Antena 3. 2009. "Doctor Mateo." Accessed March 25, 2009. http://www.antena3.com/promocional/doctormateo.

———. 2013. "Vive cantando." Accessed August 14, 2015. http://www.antena3.com/series/vive-cantando/karaoke-la-bamba/.

Armiñán, Jaime de. 1963. *Guiones de TV*. Barcelona: Rialp.

Barranco, Justo. 2014. "Y un buen día Benet i Jornet creó …" *La Vanguardia*, October 2. Accessed September 3, 2015. http://www.lavanguardia.com/television/series/20140210/54400995795/buen-dia-benet-jornet-creo.html.

Benet, Vicente J. 2012. *El cine español: una historia cultural*. Barcelona: Paidós.

Bersani, Leo. 2009. *Homos*. Cambridge, MA: Harvard University Press.

Bourdieu, Pierre. 1996. *Distinction: A Social Critique of the Judgement of Taste*. London: Routledge.

Buonanno, Milly. 2008. *The Age of Television: Experiences and Theories*. Bristol: Intellect.

———. 2014. "Quality Television and Transnational Standards." Lecture presented at Graduate Center, CUNY, November 21.

Buse, Peter, Núria Triana Toribio, and Andrew Willis. 2007. *The Cinema of Álex de la Iglesia*. Manchester: Manchester University Press.

Bustamante, Enrique. 2004. *La televisión económica*. Barcelona: Gedisa.

Caimán. 2013. Special supplement: "El otro cine español."

Castelló, Enric, Alexander Dhoest, and Hugh O'Donnell. 2009. *The Nation on Screen: Discourses of the National on Global Television*. Newcastle: Cambridge Scholars.

Castells, Manuel. 1997. *The Power of Identity*. Oxford: Blackwell.

Chica de la Tele. 2015. "¿Qué es un programa cultural?" *Chicadelatele*, March 13. Accessed September 1, 2015. http://www.chicadelatele.com/2015/03/13/que-es-un-programa-cultural.

Clubcultura 2005. "Pedro Almodóvar: Official Site." Accessed June 12, 2010. http://www.clubcultura.com/clubcine/clubcineastas/almodovar/eng/homeeng.htm.

Con el culo al aire. 2011a. "Antena 3 prepara la adaptación de 'Marco,' la serie 'Toledo,' y la comedia 'Con el culo al aire.'" Accessed August 14, 2015. http://www.formulatv.com/noticias/20358/antena3-prepara-adaptacion-pequeno-marco-serie-toledo-comedia-con-el-culo-al-aire/.

———. 2011b. "Antena 3 presenta 'Con el culo al aire,' una comedia sin pelos en la lengua, sin censuras ni tapujos." Accessed August 14, 2015. http://www.formulatv.com/noticias/21872/antena3-presenta-con-el-culo-al-aire-comedia-sin-pelos-en-la-lengua-sin-censuras/.

———. 2012. "Audiencias." Accessed August 14, 2015. http://www.formulatv.com/series/con-el-culo-al-aire/audiencias/.

———. 2014. "Sonia Martínez: 'Esta tercera temporada de "Con el culo al aire" significa que está entrando en la madurez.'" Accessed August 14, 2015. http://www.formulatv.com/noticias/36328/sonia-martinez-tercera-temporada-con-el-culo-al-aire-entrando-madurez/.

Corner, John. 1999. *Critical Ideas in Television Studies.* New York: Oxford University Press.

Crematorio. 2010a. "Pepe Sancho protagonizará 'Crematorio,' la primera serie de Canal+." Accessed August 14, 2015. http://www.formulatv.com/noticias/15219/pepe-sancho-protagonizara-crematorio-la-primera-serie-de-canal/.

———. 2010b. "'Crematorio' llegará a Canal+ el próximo mes de marzo." Accessed August 14, 2015. http://www.formulatv.com/noticias/17683/crematorio-llegara-canalplus-proximo-mes-marzo/.

———. 2011. "Miguel Salvat: 'Los actores deberían sentirse orgullosos de participar en "Crematorio."'" Accessed August 14, 2015. http://www.formulatv.com/noticias/18183/miguel-salvat-actores-sentirse-orgullosos-participar-crematorio/.

———. 2012. "Audiencias." Accessed August 14, 2015. http://www.formulatv.com/series/Crematorio/audiencias/.

De Pedro, Gonzalo, and Lourdes Monterrubio. 2009. "Servidumbres televisivas." *Cahiers du Cinéma España* 23 (May): 50.

D'Lugo, Marvin. 2006. *Pedro Almodóvar.* Urbana: University of Illinois Press.

D'Lugo, Marvin, and Kathleen M. Vernon, eds. 2013. *A Companion to Pedro Almodóvar.* Oxford: Blackwell.

Domènech, Conxita, and Andrés Lema-Hincapié (eds.). 2015. *Ventura Pons: una mirada excepcional desde el cine catalán.* Madrid: Iberoamerican/Vervuert.

Economist. 2013. "Path Dependence." Accessed November 15. http://www.economist.com/economics-a-to-z/p#node-21529571.

El Deseo. 2009. *Los abrazos rotos: A Film by Almodóvar.* Madrid: El Deseo.

Ellis, John. 2002. *Seeing Things: Television in the Age of Uncertainty.* London: I. B. Tauris.

Epps, Brad, and Despina Kakoudaki, eds. 2009. *All about Almodóvar: A Passion for Cinema.* Minneapolis: University of Minnesota Press.

Ermakoff, Ivan. 2013. "Rational Choice May Take Over." In *Bourdieu and Historical Analysis,* edited by Phillip S. Gorsky, 89–106. Durham, NC: Duke University Press.

Evans, Chris. 2010. "Giving Audiences What They Want." *Screen International,* February 5, 40–42.

Eurofiction (Milly Buonanno and the European Audiovisual Observatory). 2007. *Television Fiction in Europe.* November 18. Accessed June 6, 2010. http://www.obs. coe.int/oea_publ/eurofic/.

Farouky, Jumana. 2005. "Acceptance: One Reel at a Time." *Time,* October 10. Accessed June 12, 2010. http://www.time.com/time/europe/hero2005/almodovar.html.

Faulkner, Sally. 2013. *A History of Spanish Film: Cinema and Society 1910–2010.* London: Bloomsbury.

———. 2004. *Literary Adaptations in Spanish Cinema.* London: Tamesis.

Fecé, Josep Lluís, and Cristina Pujol. 2003. "La crisis imaginada de un cine sin público." In *Once miradas sobre la crisis y el cine español,* edited by Luis Alonso García, 147–65. Madrid: Ocho y Medio.

Fernàndez, Josep Anton. 1995. "Becoming Normal: Cultural Politics and Cultural Production in Catalonia." In *Spanish Cultural Studies,* edited by Jo Labanyi and Helen Graham, 342–46. Oxford: Oxford University Press.

Fernández Mallo, Agustín. 2009a. *Nocilla Lab.* Madrid: Alfaguara. Kindle edition.

———. 2009b. "Proyecto Nocilla, la película." Accessed September 15, 2013. http://blogs. alfaguara.com/fernandezmallo/proyecto-nocilla-la-pelicula/.

Fernández Santos, Elsa. 2008. "Bajo el volcán Almodóvar." *El País,* June 8, 40–41.

———. 2011. "25 aniversario de los Goya." *El País,* February 13. Accessed September 15, 2013. http://cultura.elpais.com/cultura/2011/02/13/actualidad/1297551601_850215. html.

FórmulaTV.com. 2009a. "'Águila roja' llenará de aventuras el prime time del jueves a partir del día 19." February 11. Accessed March 25, 2009. http://www.formulatv. com/1,20090211,10294,1.html.

———. 2009b. "'23-F' pulveriza todos los récords en su desenlace con 7 millones de espectadores." February 13. Accessed March 25, 2009. http://www.formulatv. com/1,20090213,10363,1.html.

———. 2009c. "José Corbacho: 'En estos tiempos de pesimismo siempre está bien ver gente que está peor que tú.'" February 16. Accessed March 25, 2009. http://www. formulatv.com/1,20090216,10400,1.html.

———. 2009d. "'Doctor Mateo,' el mejor estreno de ficción de Antena 3 desde 2004." February 23. Accessed March 25, 2009. http://www.formulatv. com/1,20090223,10485,1.html.

———. 2009e. "Gonzalo de Castro: 'Me parece una tontería que me comparen con House.'" February 20. Accessed March 25, 2009. http://www.formulatv. com/1,20090220,10448,1.html.

———. 2009e. "'Pelotas' debuta como segunda opción de la noche con 3.5 millones." February 24. Accessed March 25, 2009. http://www.formulatv.com/1,20090224,10491,1.html.

———. 2009f. "'Águila Roja' mantiene a sus 5 millones como la serie más vista." February 27. Accessed March 25, 2009. http://www.formulatv.com/1,20090227,10528,1.html.

———. 2009g. "'Doctor Mateo' mantiene el liderazgo, pero baja frente a 'Aída.'" March 2. Accessed March 25, 2009. http://www.formulatv.com/1,20090302,10554,1.html.

———. 2009h. "Antena 3 renueva 'Doctor Mateo' por una segunda temporada." March 17. Accessed March 25, 2009. http://www.formulatv.com/1,20090317,10751,1.html.

———. 2011a. "Un fallo en el acelerador de partículas de Ginebra, punto de inicio de 'El barco.'" January 14. Accessed September 15, 2013. http://www.formulatv.com/noticias/17915/fallo-acelerador-particulas-ginebra-inicio-el-barco/.

———. 2011b. "Foro El barco: lo de Coca Cola en El barco ya es digno de estudio." November 4. Accessed September 15, 2013. http://www.formulatv.com/series/el-barco/foros/2892/1/lo-de-la-coca-cola-en-el-barco-ya-es-digno-de-estudio-xd/.

———. 2013. "Antena 3 pondrá punto y final a 'El barco' tras su tercera temporada." February 1. Accessed September 15, 2013. http://www.formulatv.com/noticias/29216/antena3-pondra-punto-final-el-barco-t   ras-tercera-temporada.

FórmulaTV.com and Concepción Cascajosa. 2007. "Lorenzo Vilches, 'El éxito de "Betty, la fea" está en un cambio cultural de la mujer urbana.'" July 29. Accessed March 25, 2009. http://www.formulatv.com/1,20070729,5045,1.html.

Fouz-Hernández, Santiago. 2015. "La mirada homoerótica en el cine de Ventura Pons: de *Ocaña, retrat intermitent* (1978) a *Ignasi M.* (2013)." In *Ventura Pons: una mirada excepcional desde el cine catalán*, edited by Conxita Domènech and Andrés Lema-Hincapié, 305–27. Madrid: Iberoamerican/Vervuert.

Fotogramas. 2009. "Generación TV 2009." *Fotogramas* 1986 (April): 104–11.

Freixas, Pau. 2015. "Notes del director." Accessed August 8, 2015. http://www.ccma.cat/tv3/cites/notes-del-director/fitxa/107280/.

G.B. 2009. "La mejor imagen de España." *El País*, May 29, 50.

Galán, Diego. 2009. "Necrológica: Gonzalo Goicoechea, Guionista de cine y periodista." *El País*, February 17. Accessed August 15, 2015. http://elpais.com/diario/2009/02/17/necrologicas/1234825202_850215.html.

Gant, Charles. 2009. "Do the 'Right' Thing." *Sight & Sound* (June): 9.

García, Rocío. 2009. "El cine español no sobrevivirá." *El País*, December 23. Accessed June 6, 2010. http://www.elpais.com/articulo/cultura/cine/espanol/sobrevivira/elpepicul/20091223elpepicul_1/Tes.

García de Castro, Mario. 2002. *La ficción televisiva popular*. Barcelona: Gedisa.

Gaycat. 2009. "*Ventdelplà*, Gay Friendly." Accessed August 8, 2015. https://gaycat.wordpress.com/2009/04/04/ventdelpla-gay-friendly/.

Gómez, Rosario G. 2009. "Televisión pública sin anuncios." *El País*, April 15. Accessed April 20, 2009. http://www.elpais.com/articulo/sociedad/Television/publica/anuncios/elpepisoc/20090415elpepisoc_3/Tes.

Grassi, Silvia. 2016. "To Be or Not to Be: The Essentialist Paradigm in Spanish and Catalan Television's Depiction of Sexuality." *Romance Studies* 34: 64–76.

Gubbins, Michael. 2008. "Tuning into a New Era." *Screen International* (August 22): 3.

Holland, John H. 2000. *Emergence: From Chaos to Order.* Oxford: Oxford University Press.

Hopewell, John. 1986. *Out of the Past: Spanish Cinema after Franco.* London: BFI.

Jacobs, Jason, and Stephen Peacock, eds. 2013. *Television Aesthetics and Style*, New York: Bloomsbury.

James, Nick. 2008. "Who Needs Critics?" *Sight & Sound* (October): 16–26.

Kinder, Marsha. 2010. "Restoring *Los abrazos rotos.*" *Film Quarterly* (Spring): 28–33.

Labrador Méndez, Germán. 2012. "Las vidas *subprime*: la circulación de *historias de vida* como tecnología de imaginación política en la crisis española." *Hispanic Review* 80(4): 557–81.

Lacalle, Charo. 2008. *El discurso televisivo sobre la inmigración.* Barcelona: Omega.

Ley del Cine. 2007. "Ley 55/2007, de 28 de diciembre, del Cine." Accessed March 25, 2009. http://noticias.juridicas.com/base_datos/Admin/l55-2007.html.

Lindo, Elvira. 2008. "Penélope: la vida de estrella importa." *El País Semanal*, September 21, 34–44.

López, Francisca, Elena Cueto Asín, and David George, eds. 2009. *Historias de la pequeña pantalla: Representaciones históricas en la televisión de la España democrática.* Madrid: Iberoamericana.

Lyddell-Scott-Jones. 2015. *Greek English Lexicon.* Accessed September 15, 2013. http://stephanus.tlg.uci.edu/lsj/#eid=1&context=lsj.

Magnusson, Lars, ed. 2009. *The Evolution of Path Dependence.* Cheltenham: Edward Elgar.

Manrique Sabogal, Winston, and Javier Rodríguez Marcos. 2010. "Narradores sin límites." *El País*, January 30. Accessed September 15, 2013. http://elpais.com/diario/2010/01/30/babelia/1264813935_850215.html.

Marano, Hara. 2003. "Our Brain's Negative Bias." *Psychology Today*, June 20. Accessed June 12, 2010. http://www.biopsychiatry.com/depression/negbias.html.

Marcos, Natalia. 2012. "Si Shakespeare viviese hoy, escribiría para HBO." November 3. Accessed September 15, 2013. http://sociedad.elpais.com/sociedad/2012/11/02/actualidad/1351882349_528064.html.

Maxwell, Richard. 2000. "New Media Technologies in Spain: A Healthy Pluralism?" In *Contemporary Spanish Cultural Studies*, edited by Barry Jordan and Ricky Morgan-Tamosunas, 170–78. London: Arnold.

Ministerio de Cultura. n.d. "Cine y audiovisuales." Accessed June 6, 2010. http://www.mcu.es/cine/.

Mira, Alberto. 2004. *De Sodoma a Chueca: una historia cultural de la homosexualidad en España en el siglo XX.* Madrid: Egales.

———. 2008. *Miradas insumisas: gays y lesbianas en el cine.* Barcelona: Egales.

Mittell, Jason. 2015. *Complex TV: The Poetics of Contemporary Television Storytelling.* New York: New York University Press.

Moreno, Fernando. 2011. "Muere Antxon Eceiza, padre del cine vasco." *ABC*, November 16. Accessed August 15, 2015. http://www.abc.es/20111116/cultura-cine/abci-eceiza-201111160138.html.

Moreno, Vicent. 2012. "Breaking the Code: *Generación Nocilla*, New Technologies and the Marketing of Literature." Accessed September 15, 2013. http://conservancy.umn.edu/bitstream/handle/11299/182966/hiol_09_07_moreno_breaking_the_code.pdf?sequence=1&isAllowed=y.

Murray, Noeleen, ed. 2007. *Desire Lines: Space, Memory and Identity in the Post-Apartheid City*. New York: Routledge.

Naredo, José Manuel, and Antonio Montiel Márquez. 2011. *El modelo inmobilario español y su culminación en el caso valenciano*. Barcelona: Icaria.

Naredo, José Manuel, and Carlos Taibo. 2013. *De la burbuja inmobilaria al decrecimiento: causas, efectos y perspectivas de la crisis*. Madrid: Fundación Coloquio Jurídico Europeo.

Nussbaum, Martha. 2001. *Upheavals of Thought: The Intelligence of Emotions*. Cambridge: Cambridge University Press.

OBITEL. 2013. *Memoria social y ficción televisiva en países iberoamericanos*. Accessed August 17, 2015. https://blogdoobitel.files.wordpress.com/2011/04/obitel-2013-espanhol.pdf.

Ordoñez, Marcos. 2015. "Hora punta del cine español." *El País*, February 7. Accessed August 17, 2015. http://cultura.elpais.com/cultura/2015/02/04/babelia/1423068329_126196.html.

Palacio, Manuel. 2001. *Historia de la televisión en España*. Barcelona: Gedisa.

———. 2006. *Las cosas que hemos visto: 50 años y más de TVE*. Madrid: RTVE.

———. 2012. *La televisión durante la Transición española*. Madrid: Cátedra.

Patterson, Hannah. 2008. "Dealer's Choice?" *Sight & Sound* (April): 30–33.

Pavlovic, Tatjana. 2007. "Television (Hi)Stories: 'Un escaparate en cada hogar.'" *Journal of Spanish Cultural Studies* 8: 5–22.

Pellicer, Lluís. 2014. *El vicio del ladrillo: la cultura de un modelo productivo*. Madrid: Catarata.

Perlman, Allison. 2015. Review of *Wired TV: Laboring over an Interactive Future*, ed. Denise Mann. *Cinema Journal* 54(4) (Summer): 173–77.

Perriam, Chris. 2003. *Stars and Masculinities in Spanish Cinema*. Oxford: Oxford University Press.

Petho, Agnes. 2010. "Intermediality in Film: A Historiography of Methodologies." *Acta Univ. Sapientiae, Film and Media Studies*, 2. Accessed October 24, 2016. http://www.acta.sapientia.ro/acta-film/C2/film2-3.pdf.

Premios Goya. 2014. "La forja de una carrera." March 13, 2015. Accessed August 17, 2015. http://premiosgoya.academiadecine.com/actualidad/detalle.php?id=471.

Resina, Joan Ramon, and William R. Viestenz (eds.). 2012. *The New Ruralism: An Epistemology of Transformed Space*. Madrid: Iberoamericana/Vervuert.

Riambau, Esteve, and Casimiro Torreiro. 2008. *Productores en El cine español: estado, dependencias y mercado*. Madrid: Cátedra/Filmoteca Española.

Rodríguez Pastoriza, Francisco. 2003. *Cultura y televisión: Una relación de conflicto*. Barcelona: Gedisa.

Rousseau, Jean Jacques. 2015. *Lettre à d'Alembert sur les spectacles*. Accessed September 1, 2015. http://www.espace-rousseau.ch/f/textes/lettre%20à%20d'alembert%20utrecht%20corrigée.pdf.

Rueda Laffond, José Carlos, and María del Mar Chicharro Merayo. 2006. *La televisión en España 1956–2006*. Madrid: Fragua.

Rueda Laffond, José Carlos, and Carlota Coronado Ruíz. 2009. *La mirada televisiva: Ficción y representación histórica en España*. Madrid: Fragua.

Ruiz del Árbol, Maruxa. 2009. "23-F, dos visiones de un mismo día." *El País*, January 23. Accessed March 25, 2009. http://www.elpais.com/articulo/Pantallas/23F/visiones/mismo/dia/elpepirtv/20090123elpepirtv_1/Tes.

Santaolalla, Isabel. 2005. *Los "otros": Etnicidad y "raza" en el cine español*. Zaragoza: Universidad de Zaragoza.

Smith, Paul Julian. 2006a. *Television in Spain: From Franco to Almodóvar*. London: Boydell and Brewer.

———. 2006b. *Spanish Visual Culture: Cinema, Television, Internet*. Manchester: Manchester University Press.

———. 2009a. "Airless Love." *Sight & Sound* (June): 18–20.

———. 2009b. "Almodóvar's Unpublished Short Stories and the Question of Queer Auteurism." *Screen* 50: 439–49.

———. 2009c. "City Girls I: Almodóvar's Women on Film and Television." In *Spanish Screen Fiction: Between Cinema and Television*, 17–37. Liverpool: Liverpool University Press.

———. 2009d. "La distancia cultural de una adaptación entre España y Estados Unidos: *Yo soy Bea* (Telecinco) y *Ugly Betty* (ABC)." In *Mercados globales, historias nacionales*, edited by Lorenzo Vilches, 171–84. Barcelona: Gedisa.

———. 2009e. *Spanish Screen Fiction: Between Cinema and Television*. Liverpool: Liverpool University Press.

Tele 5. 2014. "Los ojos de Belén: Marruecos." February 2. Accessed August 17, 2015. http://www.telecinco.es/losojosdebelen/a-carta/ojos-Belen-Marruecos-T01xC05_2_1748280198.html.

Televisión Española. 2009. "A la carta." Accessed March 25, 2009. http://www.rtve.es/alacarta/.

Thompson, Kristin. 2003. *Storytelling in Film and Television*. Cambridge, MA: Harvard University Press.

Triana-Toribio, Núria. 2007. "Journeys of El Deseo between the Nation and the Transnational in Spanish Cinema." *Studies in Hispanic Cinemas* 4: 151–63.

———. 2008. "Auteurism and Commerce in Contemporary Spanish Cinema: *Directores Mediáticos*." *Screen* 49: 259–76.

Triper, José María. 2007. "Los servicios, 'salvavidas' de la exportación." *El País: Economía*, August 5, 11.

TV3. 2008. "VDP al descobert: Sense tabús." Video. Accessed August 8, 2015. https://www.youtube.com/watch?v=8pv3y01tX7Q.

———. 2015. "*Cites* Argument." Video. Accessed August 8, 2015. http://www.ccma.cat/tv3/cites/argument/fitxa/107140/.

Vanity Fair. 2009. "Íntimo y secreto," April. Accessed June 12, 2010. http://cinefille.blogspot.com/2009/03/penelope-cruz-and-pedro-almodovar-in.html.

Vernon, Kathleen M. 2007. "Las canciones de Almodóvar." In *Hispanismo y cine*, edited by Javier Herrera and Cristina Martínez-Carazo, 241–56. Madrid: Iberoamericana.

Vidal, Nuria. 1989. *El cine de Pedro Almodóvar*. Barcelona: Destino.

Vilches, Lorenzo. 2007. *Culturas y mercados de la ficción televisiva en Iberoamérica.* Barcelona: Gedisa.

———. 2009. "La audiencia de TV en febrero 2009." Accessed March 25, 2009. http://antalya.uab.es/guionactualidad/IMG/pdf/Mensual_2009_02.pdf.

Vive cantando. 2013a. "María Castro salta a Antena 3 para protagonizar la comedia 'Vivo [*sic*] cantando.'" Accessed August 14, 2015. http://www.formulatv.com/noticias/29763/maria-castro-salta-antena3-protagonizar-vivo-cantando/.

———. 2013b. "Así son los personajes de 'Vivo [*sic*] cantando,' la nueva comedia dramática de Antena 3." Accessed August 14, 2015. http://www.formulatv.com/noticias/31434/personajes-vivo-cantando-nueva-comedia-dramatica-antena3/.

———. 2014. "Antena 3 no renueva 'Vive cantando' por una tercera temporada." Accessed August 14, 2015. http://www.formulatv.com/noticias/40876/antena-3-no-renueva-vive-cantando-tercera-temporada/.

Wikipedia. 2010a. "Pedro Almodóvar [English]." Accessed June 12, 2010. http://en.wikipedia.org/wiki/Pedro_Almodóvar.

———. 2010b. "Pedro Almodóvar [French]." Accessed June 12, 2010. http://fr.wikipedia.org/wiki/Pedro_Almodóvar.

———. 2010c. "Pedro Almodóvar [Spanish]." Accessed June 12, 2010. http://es.wikipedia.org/wiki/Pedro_Almodóvar.

YouTube. 2009. "Águila Roja, adelanto en exclusiva del capítulo 2." Accessed March 25, 2009. http://www.youtube.com/watch?v=E8z1L8ZFq9k&feature=related.

Zurián, Francisco A., et al., eds. 2005. *Almodóvar: el cine como pasión*. Cuenca: Universidad de Castilla-La Mancha.

Index